Table of Contents

Oh Cancer, My Cancer: A Memoir

Christopher Spevack

Oh Cancer, My Cancer: A Memoir

Copyright © 2016 by Christopher Spevack

Cover Design by Wayne Molinare
Edited by Jennifer Barrows and Cher Johnson

To contact the author, visit
CMS376@yahoo.com

ISBN 978-0-9962767-0-2

Printed in the United States of America

Dedication

To the victims and survivors of cancer: past, present and future, and the caregivers who support them in the fight.

Acknowledgments

To my mother: guardian angel, source of strength and guidance throughout my cancer journey. I love you with all of my heart and I am eternally grateful for your love, support and devotion.

To my father, for lovingly providing for and supporting our family. Thank you for always being there. Your dedication was instrumental to my healing.

To my sister, for treating me like a normal brother instead of a cancer patient. Thank you for never treating me differently, and for caring and helping me during my fight.

To the doctors, nurses, therapists, technologists and teachers who actively participated in my care. Thank you all for saving my life.

To my wife, for supporting me throughout the writing process. Thank you for listening to every word, and encouraging me during the highs and lows of this journey. I love you.

To my uncle Wayne, for your time, patience and creativity in designing an amazing book cover and brand logo.

To Drew Smith, for introducing me to publishing at an early age, and for your encouraging words and critique in this new endeavor.

There are so many people to thank for their participation in my cancer ordeal. I wouldn't know where to begin. For this reason, I have chosen not to include names in the book, for fear of leaving out someone very important to my story. I treasure you all in my hearts always and thank you for everything you did for me and my family.

Foreword

I still remember walking into Chris's hospital room soon after his diagnosis of a malignant brain tumor. A very sick and frightened adolescent, he was facing a rigorous treatment regimen of radiation and chemotherapy. I have witnessed his struggles and his strength and, with his family, friends and other medical staff, supported him as he overcame the many challenges that confronted him. Now Chris has dedicated himself to helping others, promoting the health, well-being and confidence of other cancer survivors, and hoping to inspire them to find the strength to overcome their challenges. I know that Chris inspires me and I believe he will inspire anyone who reads his story.

With advances in diagnosis and treatment, more children and adolescents are surviving cancer than ever before. But the cure may come with a price, especially for teenagers who are also trying to cope with the difficult tasks of growing up. In addition to dealing with potential side effects from the treatment, the isolation from their peers and the inability to attend school can have a profound effect upon their emotional well-being and psychological growth.

Chris's story is a compelling testament to the power of the human spirit. Not only did Chris endure, he persevered. Not only did he survive, he triumphed over great medical and personal challenges to become a compassionate and caring man, demonstrating tremendous resilience and courage in the face of adversity.

His story is meaningful and important not only for other young people battling cancer, but also for the family, friends and medical personnel who care for them as they fight for their lives and their successful future.

Cathy Shimmel RN MA CPON

Introduction

I was twelve years old. It was August 9th, 1988. My mom and dad had just received horrible news about my tests. I sat in complete confusion and looked to them for some understanding. I had no idea they had just received the most devastating news that would affect all of our lives.

I am a cancer survivor of medulloblastoma, an aggressive, highly metastatic malignant brain tumor. I successfully underwent sixteen months of treatment, consisting of surgery, radiation and chemotherapy and remain in remission since completion in January 1990. I have accomplished many great things, achieving my own American dream. I graduated college, have a good job, got married, bought a house and live happily with my wife Christine and two dogs, Fifi and Gretel.

My cancer experience was without a doubt terrifying and life-changing. I have often questioned why I was so blessed when others were not so fortunate. Why was I still around when others perished? Why was I so lucky when others succumbed to their illnesses? Questions, thoughts and emotions often clash within my mind as I struggle with my mortality and purpose in this world. Yet one thing is certain, I appreciate each day I have on this earth and am thankful to be alive.

Regretfully, I have lost touch with many survivors from my past. Perhaps we drifted apart, no longer restrained to an unwelcome bond. Maybe we simply moved on, haunted by our pasts, troubled by an uncertain future, tormented by a stigma that will follow us forever. Whatever the case, I hope they are healthy and well, surviving and thriving in life. They will forever remain close to my heart.

Cancer is a vicious predator, restless and unforgiving. There is no remorse, sympathy or compassion for the fatalities left in its path. Cancer simply attacks without pity, mercy, or understanding. It continues to destroy families, manipulating human life and claiming thousands of American lives each year. It flourishes, infects and remains victorious as we still search for the cure. Cancer is a time bomb that remains ticking as we attempt to rid the world of this deadly disease.

My goal for this book is to bring awareness and help people understand the complexities of cancer and the emotional rollercoaster ride that unfolds. I share personal accounts of my journey to show that having cancer is not always a losing battle and that life does not have to end because of it. I will show that cancer, although scary, daunting and difficult, can be conquered.

My intent is to help change lives, one person at a time. If this book motivates just one person to push a little further, dig a little deeper or fight a little harder, then I will be grateful to have touched someone in a positive way. I hope my story inspires you to overcome personal adversities, knowing that cancer is not a death sentence. I invite you to read on and discover the highs and lows, the struggles within and the miraculous breakthroughs discovered along the path to recovery.

Carpe Diem "Seize the Day."

Horace

Yesterday, all my troubles seemed so far away.

The Beatles

1

Beep...Beep...Beep... I could hear the heart monitor as I awoke from my brief rest. I opened my eyes and sat up in my hospital bed. I had just fallen asleep. "Oh no, not again." I moaned. "Already?" I could feel the waves of nausea rise up into my esophagus and enter my throat. "Where is the damn bowl?" I thought to myself. "I just used it!" I scrambled to find the small crescent shaped emesis bowl that lay near my bedside. "Someone must have moved it when I fell asleep." I assumed. "It was just washed and placed on the table next to my bed. I hope I don't make a mess again." I winced.

I frantically searched my surroundings for the bowl as the churning inside my stomach intensified. I was going to throw up again. Mom ran over to the bed to help me. "Chris, the bowl is right next to your leg!" she yelled. She knew what was happening and came to assist. I reached over to pick up the emesis bowl and got into position. I couldn't stop it. I began to tense up. I leaned forward, closed my eyes and opened my mouth.

I heaved once...nothing happened. I heaved again...this one hurt, as I felt a cramp form in my chest...still nothing. I heaved a third time and brown fluid splashed into the bowl - just bile. I coughed and gagged, spitting phlegm into the container. No mess this time.

The waves of nausea dissipated and my body began to relax. The heaving had finally stopped. Mom took the emesis bowl and headed to the bathroom to dispose of the contents. She rinsed it out and placed it next to me on the bed. I asked her for the box of tissues on the bedside table so I could blow my nose and clean my mouth. I leaned back in bed, turned on my side and placed my head on the pillow, attempting to get comfortable again. "Mom, what time is it?" I asked. She replied, "It's 1:37 in the morning honey. Try to go back to sleep. The bag is almost empty and you are almost done. No more after this!"

I had been vomiting all day from the chemotherapy I was receiving. Ironically, the cancer fighting medicine required for my survival was killing me from within. That was episode number eleven, according to my count. "At least it will be over soon," I sighed. "No more chemotherapy after this." The doctor had said that I had enough. I could go home in a few hours, my chemo finally completed. Mom tucked me into bed placing the bed sheet over my thin, cold, shaking body. It had been a long night.

I closed my eyes and prayed I wouldn't puke again. I was physically exhausted. I tried to think happy thoughts so I could quickly fall back to sleep. I repeated over and over to myself, "Please, let me get some rest. No more disruptions." As I drifted off, I thought about the long road I had taken to get to this point.

Sometimes you get to choose your battles and sometimes they choose you.

Gabe Gruenwald

2

I completed my first year of middle school. I made some new friends, had my first crush and broke some hearts. I made some remarkable discoveries about myself and made some poor decisions. I was living life, making choices, learning. I was approaching my teenage years and life was changing.

I was a popular kid in elementary school, active in school activities. The guys hung out with me, while the girls swarmed around me. They would chase me around the school yard, my buddies pushing them away. I had many admirers and even a girlfriend. I graduated at the top of my class, Hamptonian of the year (similar to Valedictorian). I was a cute kid—smart, athletic and funny, living the best years of my life.

When I wasn't in school I was outside playing with kids on my block. I was never in the house and my mom always had to track me down for dinner. I often quickly devoured my meals and went right out the door looking for someone to play with. I entertained myself for hours from dusk 'till dawn.

Sports were my passion. I played them, I watched them and I excelled at them. Posters of favorite players lined my bedroom walls. I collected baseball cards and sticker albums, and attended hockey and baseball games with my dad.

I had dreams of becoming a professional athlete, pretending to hit that game winning home run or score the winning goal. I worshipped my sport heroes and tried to be just like them. I played baseball and soccer for the local athletic association and bowled regularly. I was a very fast runner with good hand-eye coordination and natural talent, performing well on and off the field.

The headaches began during Father's Day weekend. I remember, because I thought they were brought on by stress. Final exams were approaching and I was nervous, hoping to pass all my tests to move on to the seventh grade. Fortunately, I passed my exams and the school year ended, but the headaches continued.

My mother, the worrier that she was, decided to make an appointment with our family pediatrician. I was examined in his office a few days later. He couldn't find anything wrong with me, and told my mother to contact him if the headaches persisted. I honestly wasn't worried. I was done with school and looked forward to enjoying my summer vacation. I figured at some point the headaches would just go away and that would be the end of it.

Summer began like most others; playing with my sister, hanging out with friends, swimming at the community pool. I attended summer recreation camp at the local park a few blocks from my house. We played games like kickball and freeze tag, and created various arts and crafts. With two months of freedom, no homework, no studying or tests, I couldn't understand why I was still getting headaches.

At first they were nothing more than an inconvenience to my summer. I would go home and lie down in my bedroom, lower the window shades and turn on the air conditioner. A few hours later I would wake up as good as new and continue my everyday routine. The headaches, however, lingered. I was beginning to get annoyed.

I then began experiencing other symptoms — blurred and double vision. This seemed unusual and so I told my mother about them. "Hey mom, I am having trouble seeing clearly. My vision is blurry and when I lay down I am seeing double."

She replied, "Let's call the pediatrician again. You've had headaches all summer and I want to get some answers about these other symptoms you have now."

Mom called the doctor right away and described at length the many symptoms I exhibited over the last few weeks. "I am worried about Chris. His headaches have continued and he is now having problems with his vision. I have noticed changes in his behavior and think something might be wrong. I think he needs to see a specialist."

The pediatrician agreed and told her to contact a neurologist. Mom contacted numerous doctors, but was unable to secure an appointment right away. Determined to have me see someone sooner than later, she decided to take me to other specialists.

Over the next six weeks I would visit an internist, ophthalmologist, an allergist and even a dermatologist. My mother took me to any doctor that would see me right away. I was troubled by the numerous trips to the doctor. My summer vacation was flying by and would soon be over. The appointments were interrupting my play time and enjoyment with friends.

I asked my mother, "How many doctors are we going to have to see before knowing what's wrong with me? These visits are taking time out of my summer fun."

Mom responded, "We need to determine why you are having so many headaches so we can fix the problem. Your father and I are worried about you and want to make sure you are okay."

"Oh, mom… I'm fine." I said, brushing it off as no big deal. I wasn't happy about the constant interruptions to my vacation, but I too was frustrated that nobody seemed to know what was going on with me. I figured someone should have an answer by now and I was getting impatient.

The visit to the allergist would point us in the right direction. During my appointment the doctor requested I go for a sinus scan. She prescribed medication for my headaches because she thought I had a problem with allergies and diagnosed me with sinusitis. She called with the results of my scan a few days later and suggested I go see a neurologist. Thankfully, the allergist was able to secure an appointment for me the next day. We were finally getting somewhere.

I remember we had the last appointment of the day. The neurologist spoke with me about my symptoms and then took me into another room for an examination. He had me walk a straight line, moving towards and away from him. He then checked my reflexes, strength and breathing. He pulled out a small flashlight from his pocket and shined it in my ears, eyes and mouth. He checked my eyes for a second time and then called his partner into the room.

"Had he discovered something?" I wondered. "Was I finally going to get some answers?" It had been weeks without an explanation and I was relieved I would soon receive some long overdue closure regarding my headaches. He had detected that something was in fact wrong. He explained that my pupils were fluttering, dancing from left to right. It was called nystagmus, a rapid eye movement. That moment would change my life forever.

Hamptonian of the Year.

A hero is an ordinary individual who finds the strength to persevere and endure in spite of overwhelming obstacles.

Christopher Reeve

3

The neurologist urgently phoned the hospital and informed them I was coming to the emergency room and that he was meeting us there. It was late in the evening and I remember him screaming at the attendant on the phone about the severity of the issue. He wanted x-rays taken of my brain to see what was happening inside my head. He yelled instructions for the doctor to stay late and to instruct the technician to stay as well to prep the CAT scan machine for me.

"What is going on?" I thought. I looked at my parents for an explanation but they were just as surprised. Things were happening very quickly and I wondered what the rush was all about. The doctor's sudden change in behavior frightened me.

The neurologist ran back and forth from his office to his secretary's desk. I didn't know what he was doing, but he was scaring me. I really wanted to go home and tell my folks to find another doctor. He rushed back into his office and looked at us and said, "I need you to head over to the hospital right now! It is down the road at the bottom of the hill. I will meet you there."

We left his office in silence, deep in thought, not knowing what was to come. I was frightened and confused and desperately wanted to go home. Couldn't we just sleep on this and decide what to do in the morning? The neurologist seemed very worried. Struck by panic and fear, my parents and I headed to the hospital. This had become very serious.

It only took five minutes to get to the emergency room. My name was called immediately and I was terrified. My parents stood up with me and we followed the nurse who had just called my name. She told my parents to wait while I was led into a changing room and instructed to remove my clothes, except for my underwear. She handed me a gown to wrap around my body.

We then continued to follow her down the hallway. I shivered as I walked down the corridor barefoot and half naked. My parents were again told to wait while I walked with the nurse toward another room. I immediately turned my head to see my parents. "Wait. They aren't coming with me?" I questioned. "I don't want to be alone! I want my mom and dad with me!" The nurse answered, "Your parents have to wait outside until your procedure is over. Then they can come in and see you."

Just then my father yelled out, "Don't worry son, it will be alright." His arm was wrapped around my mother. "It will be okay Chris. We will be right here." Mom acknowledged. I followed the nurse into the room and was instructed to get onto the exam table and lay flat on my back.

I stared up at the ceiling, wondering what was to happen next. Suddenly, the entrance door opened and I peered over to see a woman walking towards me. I stared at her, observing the yellow outfit she was wearing and the box in her right hand. My eyes immediately detected the pointy needles inside. "Are those for me?" I asked out loud, fearing the obvious answer. "What is happening now?" I questioned. Who was this person? The nurse explained that the woman was a phlebotomist and she would be placing an I.V. into my arm.

The phlebotomist placed the box down next to me and said hello. I responded and questioned, "Why do I have to get a needle?" She said, "You are going to have some pictures taken of the inside of your head and a contrast dye is required for the procedure." I then asked, "Is the needle going to hurt? I never had something like this done before." She clarified, "You may feel a slight pinch."

My entire body began to tremble. I wasn't comfortable with this at all. I had never been stuck with an I.V. needle before and I was afraid. Besides, the only pain I experienced as a young kid came from sports injuries, and cuts and scrapes from playing outside. I didn't want a needle and I was petrified.

My eyes began to well up with tears, dripping down both of my cheeks. The phlebotomist saw how afraid I was and tried to console me. She said, "I have done this hundreds of times. It will be quick and painless. Take a few breaths and try to relax." I believed her and took a few moments to compose myself and told her I was ready.

She began probing my arms for a good vein — first my right, then left. Once she found a "winner," she swabbed the area with an alcohol wipe. I was told to make a fist while she tied a tourniquet around my bicep. She then began to press her finger on the vein in preparation to stick me. My anxiety increased and my body tensed as the needle moved closer and closer to my skin. I just wanted it to be over and done with.

I asked her, "Could you please count to three before putting the needle into my arm? This way I know exactly when the needle will stick my skin and I can prepare for the pinch." She replied, "Of course." She slowly began to count.

I closed both eyes and turned my head the other way. I couldn't bear to watch the needle go into my arm. "One...Two...Three..." The needle was in. "Wow!" I exclaimed. "That didn't hurt at all." I was relieved it was over.

The phlebotomist placed some gauze over the needle with some adhesive tape so the needle wouldn't move while the dye was administered. I was told to keep my arm straight and motionless on the table while she connected the bag of dye to my I.V. I watched as the clear fluid trickled down towards my arm. I breathed in a sigh of relief, pleased my first I.V. needle experience had gone so well. Little did I know it would be the first of many over the next several months!

I lay motionless on the table as the contrast dye flowed through my veins and into my body. The nurse and phlebotomist left the room so the tests could begin and I was now alone. My parents watched from the adjoining room.

Only a minute or two had passed when I began feeling a warm sensation where the needle pierced my skin. I suddenly had difficulty breathing and began to wheeze and struggle for breath. I remember thinking, "Oh my God, oh my God, what is happening? Someone please help me!" My mind began to race and I started to panic.

Suddenly the entrance door opened and a doctor and nurse ran towards me. The doctor placed an oxygen mask over my nose and mouth, while the nurse removed the I.V. from my arm. I was frightened and gasped for air while tears poured down my face.

I couldn't see my parents, my view obstructed by the doctor and nurse assisting me. I wanted them here in the room with me to make it all better, just like they always did when I was scared or in pain. I imagined how scared and helpless they must have felt, watching the events unfold from the other room – their son struggling to breathe.

I was told to sit up on the table while the doctor instructed me to breathe deeply into the mask. I could feel the oxygen enter my nasal passages and seep into my lungs. It was then I noticed my parents had entered the room. They had tears in their eyes and concerned looks on their faces, as they watched helplessly while the doctor and nurse assisted me.

"What the hell happened?" my father screamed. He was very protective and had been on edge ever since we left the neurologist's office a few hours earlier. The doctor explained, "Your son had an allergic reaction to the contrast dye." Dad continued his rant. "My son could have died right here on the table!" My father had never liked doctors and the recent events not only angered him but added to his already high anxiety.

The doctor re-directed his attention to me. "Are you breathing okay now?" he asked. "Are you feeling any better?" I nodded yes. He continued, "I am going to take the oxygen mask off. Try to relax and take a few minutes to catch your breath. We will resume the testing when you are ready."

The doctor removed the mask from my face and gave me some time to calm down. I wiped the tears away from my face and took some deep breaths. I returned to my original position as everyone exited the room. Testing began once again but without the contrast dye. It would be the first and last time I would ever receive it. I clearly was not off to a very good start.

Let's play some soccer!

You have to fight through some bad days to earn the best days of your life.

Anonymous

4

I was cold and afraid. I tried to stay as still as possible, but could not stop shaking from nerves and fear. I kept wondering what was going on in the other room and when the tests would be over. I hoped everything would be fine so I could get out of here and go home. I was ready to leave this place.

My parents came into the exam room once the tests were over. Mom spoke first. "Chris, you are going to be fine. If the tests show anything, we will deal with it as a family." Dad followed, "You will be okay son. We love you." I grabbed mom and dad by the hands and took a deep breath, closed my eyes and prayed that nothing was wrong with my tests.

Minutes later the neurologist walked in. His furrowed brow and somber look revealed his diagnosis before his words did. "Chris, I need to speak with your parents a moment. One of the nurses will wait here with you." My parents were taken into another room.

Images of my brain were displayed on various monitors. The doctor showed the pictures to my parents and pointed to one in particular that revealed a golf ball sized lump on the back of my brain. He said, "That is a tumor in your son's brain, and it needs to come out right away. Your

17

son is very sick." He continued. "Chris' scans reveal a high grade metastatic tumor in his brain called medulloblastoma, and it is malignant. Your son has cancer", explained the doctor.

My parents gasped. Tears were pouring down my mother's cheeks. My father immediately stood up and said we were going home, however, Mom began questioning the neurologist about my diagnosis.

"What happens now?" she asked frantically. "How sick is my son? Where do we go from here?"

The doctor explained, "Your son has a very aggressive tumor in his head and surgery will be required, as well as radiation and chemotherapy. He will need to be..." Mom interrupted him mid-sentence, her voice now louder than before. "How are you so sure you need to do these invasive procedures on my son? Maybe you are mistaken?" My father jumped in at this point and said, "We would like to get a second opinion."

Dad was ready to leave. He had heard enough and turned to my mother. "Let's go! We are getting out of here!" My mother got up to follow him. The neurologist pleaded with my folks to reconsider. "Wait! You cannot leave. Your son has a serious health condition and needs treatment right away!"

Mom turned around to face him and asked, "What would happen if I remove my son from the hospital and bring him home?" The neurologist was insistent, "Your son is sick and can possibly suffer a stroke or go into a coma. If you leave with him, I will call the cops and have you arrested for child endangerment. Your son has a life threatening illness and his life is in jeopardy."

I don't think my parents were prepared to hear such devastating news from the doctor. In hindsight, I believe my parents feared something was wrong, as I had been to so many doctors without an explanation for my headaches. However I don't think they ever imagined my diagnosis to be this severe!

While my parents spoke with the doctor about my condition, the nurse assisted me off the exam table. She led me to the changing room so I could remove the gown and put my clothes back on. I just sat there silent in a state of confusion and total disbelief. This wasn't making any sense. I hadn't done anything wrong. "Why was this happening to me?" I pondered. "Was I sick? Could I die? What was going to happen to me?" I feared.

The nurse then escorted me back outside where my parents anxiously awaited my return. They pulled me in close for another embrace, my recent brush with death still fresh.

I was scared and couldn't stop shaking. "What happens now?" I wondered. "Can I go home after this?" I turned to my parents and asked, "Is something wrong with me? Am I going to be okay?" They placed their hands on my shoulders, pulling me in close once again. I looked at their faces and saw the uncertainty. Perhaps they knew something already and were just trying to protect me.

As I struggled to wrap my head around recent events, I couldn't help but shift my thoughts to my little sister Tara. She was staying at a neighbor's house so my parents could take me to the doctor. Tara was nine years old, knew quite well about my headaches and was worried about me.

I wondered what she was doing at that moment. Was she eating dinner? Was she playing and having fun? Was she thinking about me? I knew she was concerned, as she watched me struggle with headaches all summer. I was often stuck in the house while she played outside with her friends.

Recently she had been staying with relatives and friends while Mom took me to doctor appointments over the past few weeks. My father worked full time but happened to take vacation this week to spend time with us and have some fun. We had just gone fishing the day before and Tara had caught the most fish! I was relieved she wasn't here now, witnessing the family collapse as we prepared for the unknown.

I was excited and hopeful that everything was okay and that we were going home. However, that would not be the case. My mother would tell me that I was sick and had to be admitted to the hospital.

"Admitted to the hospital? Why do I have to be admitted? I want to go home! I don't want to be in the hospital!" Tears began pouring from my eyes once again, and I began to shake uncontrollably. I was frightened beyond words. My parents clutched me tight as we all cried together. Now that we had an answer we could prepare for the uncertain, but first someone was going to have to tell Tara.

Mom stayed with me at the hospital while dad drove back home to pick up my sister. Dad stopped home with her before returning to the hospital. While entering the house, she asked, "Dad, where is Chris? Where is Mom? Is everything okay?"

Dad turned to her and said, "Your brother is very sick and he could die. He has to stay in the hospital for surgery." She followed him as he walked through the kitchen down the hallway into his bedroom, where he dropped to his knees and brought both hands to his face and sobbed. It was the first time my sister had ever seen him cry.

Meanwhile, back in the emergency room, tears continued to flow as Mom and I cried together. I couldn't accept that something was wrong with me and that my life was at risk. I wondered if this was just a bad dream I was having or some sort of cruel joke. I thought, "This isn't really happening, right? School starts in less than a month and soccer tryouts begin soon. I have summer camp to finish and friends to play with and my life to live. *This* was not part of the plan."

The neurologist admitted me that night into pediatric intensive care. I was placed in a private room and hooked up to a heart monitor and I.V. drip. Nurses monitored my blood pressure and temperature, recording numbers and results onto a clipboard that hung on the door of my room. I was subjected to numerous tests, including an MRI and a second CAT scan. For the next two days I was studied like a lab rat, analyzed and critiqued by several doctors.

I was frightened by all the unfamiliar faces and desperately wanted to go home. The next forty-eight hours were the scariest and most terrifying of my entire life. I had no idea who they were or what was going to happen to me. Little did I realize at the time, they were making essential preparations for what would soon become the hardest two years of my existence.

I was sitting in bed watching television when the neurologist entered my room. He asked me how I was feeling and I told him I was fine. The truth was I wasn't fine. I was terrified beyond words and absolutely clueless about what had transpired over the last few days. He motioned to my parents and they left the room, closing the door. I watched them from my bed, but could not hear their conversation.

The neurologist would tell them, "Your son will need to undergo surgery right away to remove his tumor and then he will need to stay in the hospital for observation. He will need to be carefully monitored and evaluated and will be placed on machines to help him breathe."

I observed the discussion from inside my room. In one moment the doctor was talking, and then my parents were crying. I wondered what they were talking about and what was going to happen to me. I could only assume my parents heard more bad news about my situation. "How the hell did this happen?" I marveled. "I'm not prepared for any of this. What a traumatic turn of events."

A week that had begun with laughter and fun had turned into dread, gloom and trepidation. My life was changing and there was nothing I could do about it. I wanted to go home and pretend this never happened. My fate was now in the hands of the doctors and I would need to have an operation. It was all too much, too sudden.

Happier times.

You never know how strong you are until being strong is the only choice you have.

Anonymous

5

How do you explain cancer to a child? The past two days were full of new developments and lots of activity. My parents had to inform me of my pending surgery. Mom would be the one to break the news. She always had a knack for explaining things so I could understand, and this time would be no different. So much had happened so fast I honestly could not keep up. I just followed orders and did what I was told to do while my mother listened and advocated on my behalf.

I lay in my hospital bed while Mom held my hand. Dad sat in a chair right beside me. The three of us were alone and I asked, "Mom, what is wrong with me? What do the doctors plan to do?" Mom leaned closer to the bed. She said, "Chris, you are very sick and the doctors are going to take something out of your head so you feel better and make the headaches go away."

"Do I need to have an operation?" I asked. "Will it hurt? Can I go home after it is done?" I had obviously not fully grasped the imminent danger I was in, nor the changes that would soon occur in my life. Mom replied, "Yes honey, you will need to have surgery. They will put you to sleep so the procedure won't hurt, but you may be in discomfort when you wake up. You will need to stay in the hospital to recover from the operation."

I didn't know how to respond. I only knew that I couldn't resume a normal life without dealing with what was in front of me right now. I was very frightened, but knew there was nothing I could say or do to change my sudden misfortune. My life hung in the balance and I had to accept the hand I was dealt and move forward against my new adversary.

I looked deep into my mothers' eyes, shattered by her explanation, and responded with every bit of honesty and simplicity that a young, scared little boy could. I said, "Ok Mom, let them get it out so I can go back to school and play with my friends."

Doctors removed my tumor on August 11th, 1988, less than forty-eight hours after diagnosis. I awoke from surgery to total darkness. My head and neck were wrapped in gauze and bandages. A breathing tube had been inserted down my throat, preventing me from speaking. An I.V. pumped fluids into one arm while a blood pressure cuff took vital signs on the other. Both wrists were Velcro® strapped to the bed. I wasn't leaving the hospital anytime soon.

My operation lasted four and a half hours. The surgeon came to my room to speak with my parents and told them, "The surgery went very well. Your son's tumor was intact and completely removed from his brain. There were no signs the tumor spread to other parts of his body. His cancer was contained."

Mom told me after the surgeon had left that the surgery was successful and I was happy the procedure went well.

However, my present condition prevented me from jumping up and down in celebration. I felt like I was hit by a truck.

All I could think about was feeling better and returning to the kid I was before my operation. I looked forward to getting out of bed and out of the hospital. I figured my nightmare would soon be over, and that I could resume my normal life and return to school in September once I recovered from the procedure. I would soon discover that recovery from a surgery like mine could take weeks.

The struggle you are in today is developing the strength you need for tomorrow.

Anonymous

6

I remained in bed for days unable to move, see or speak. I was completely terrified. Stricken with fear, I cried and flailed in desperation for help. I was so afraid and helpless, unable to communicate with my loved ones. I could only hear their voices and that at least kept my mind at ease.

I spent days with my eyes closed trying to sleep. I figured I might as well pass the time dreaming rather than sitting in agony doing absolutely nothing. I visualized myself at home playing outside and hanging out with all of my friends. Sadly, I would awake disappointed and trapped in my present reality, confined to a hospital bed with nowhere to go. Hours I thought were spent in slumber turned out to be only minutes.

Doctors frequently checked on my condition so I was constantly interrupted. Nurses would disturb me to take my blood pressure and temperature or change an empty I.V. bag or stick me with a needle to receive more blood. It seemed like anyone and everyone entered my room to bother me and disrupt my privacy. It became quite annoying.

I desperately wanted to express how I felt, so they could hear me yell and complain about how pissed off I was and how much pain I was in. I wanted to tell them to leave me alone and to stay the hell away from me. All I wanted to do was rest and go home.

I was in excruciating pain and discomfort from surgery. My throat was sore and I had difficulty breathing. I couldn't see a thing and I wasn't able to move. My head was killing me - someone had taken a knife and cut it open! All I could do was lay in bed, rest and pray for some improvement in my condition.

My family would help me in any way they could. They held my hands as I drifted in and out of sleep and would cover me with blankets when I got cold. They would sit next to my bed and talk to me to help pass the time, and put the TV on so I could listen to a program. Since I couldn't eat or drink they would feed me ice chips or squeeze water from a soaked wash-cloth into my mouth. There were even times when they had to help me go to the bathroom since I couldn't get out of bed! They did whatever was necessary to keep me comfortable.

I certainly didn't want to be in the hospital. I wanted to be home playing with my friends. I wanted to be anywhere else besides this uncomfortable bed and in this predicament. My identity had shifted from a very healthy boy to a very sick one. I was unable to do much of anything but wait further instructions regarding my care. I desperately wanted out of this situation, stuck here against my wishes, unable to be a kid.

Days would pass with no change in my condition. I was beginning to get fidgety, confined to my bed, unable to get up and move around. I was agitated and limited against my will and yearned for some relief.

My mother spoke to the neurologist during one of his visits. "How long will Chris be unable to see? When will the breathing tube come out? Can the straps come off his wrists? He is so uncomfortable." He explained; "Chris' vision impairment is only temporary and will return. The breathing tube and straps will need to remain for a little longer as precaution and can be removed once his condition improves."

The neurologist held all the cards in the deck and I simply had no control over anything happening in my life. I was furious and wanted to tell him how much I hated him. I wanted to scream at him for ruining my life and putting me here! I wanted *him* to be trapped in this hospital bed, not me.

I would learn very early in my treatment that patience would become my most valuable asset. I had no other option but deal with my current situation. I was miserable, yet I realized complaining would not change my current status. I had to be patient and let time heal my wounds and wait for further improvement. I would simply have to ride out the storm.

After ten days in the hospital, I finally began showing signs of improvement. The doctor removed my breathing tube and the Velcro® straps from my wrists so I was finally able to get up and move around. This was a huge relief to no longer feel like a hostage, and more like a patient. The nurses also removed the bandages from the back of my head.

My eyesight slowly returned but remained blurry for some time. I could see colors and shapes again, but struggled with some double vision. At least I wasn't living in complete darkness anymore.

I soon discovered I could see more clearly if I covered my left eye and favored my right. I began holding a towel over my eye but my arm began to hurt from holding it in place. My grandfather; the inventor that he was, came up with a clever idea. He took a pair of plastic sunglasses and popped out the lenses. He then inserted an eye patch into the left lens and replaced it back into the frame, leaving the right section open. I no longer had to hold anything in front of my eye and could now wear the glasses on my face to see.

I was so afraid of what I would see and the damage the doctors had done to my appearance. I remember touching the wound for the first time; the skin still soft and extremely delicate to the touch. My head had been shaved, as I could no longer feel hair on the back of my head and neck.

The stiches crossed in an X pattern down the back of my head, the metal hard and cold to the touch. I could feel the gaps where the stitch met the skin as I rubbed a finger up and down the incision. It was so gross that my body cringed and my arm shook, startled that my once smooth skull now felt butchered and disfigured.

I had to see what it looked like. Now that I could get up, I asked my mother to help me into the bathroom to see myself in the mirror. I couldn't turn my neck and head much from the surgery and soreness, so I asked my mother if she had a mirror I could use to catch a glimpse of the incision.

She removed a small makeup mirror from her purse and aimed it at the bathroom mirror to reflect the image of the back of my head. I gasped. There in the reflection I could see a long vertical scar with multiple staples down the entire stitch. It was terrifying and I quickly looked away in complete and utter shock. I was distraught, horrified by what I saw. It looked like someone just constructed a railroad track on the back of my head!

I freaked out. "Everyone is going to notice this!" I yelled. "What are they going to think and say when they see me? It looks like a mangled, twisted wreck back there."

I felt like I was going to collapse. This was all too much for me to bear. I couldn't believe what the surgery had done to my appearance. I never expected anything like this!

The severity of my illness hit me full force right then and there. I had been cut open and sewn back together; left with a permanent mark that would remain with me forever! Heartbroken and disgusted, I slowly returned to my hospital bed. I was so upset and unhappy at what I had just observed. Unfortunately for me it had to be done, and as disappointed as I felt, I knew it was necessary in order to save my life.

My parents would reveal the whole truth about my condition a few days after surgery. Sitting at my bedside, they told me that I had cancer, and explained to me that I had a malignant brain tumor called medulloblastoma and that I could have died.

My jaw instantly dropped open and my heart sank. I sat there quiet, unsure how to react. I was confused. "What is a tumor? What is cancer?" I thought to myself. "What is medulla...what was it called? I had no idea what my parents had just told me and looked to them for some understanding.

Mom said, "We are just as confused as you are Chris, but we have to do what the doctors say so you will get well. We will take it one day at a time." I couldn't help but feel so lost and uncertain, and prayed there would be no more bad news.

Since I was making progress, I was finally allowed to have visitors at the hospital. I was so happy to see friends and people from my neighborhood. Initially, many of them were shocked to see me in my current condition. Everything had happened so fast between my diagnosis and then the surgery that many of them had no idea why I was in the hospital. But one look at me and it was evident I had been through a war.

I listened to them as they spoke with my parents. "Oh my God, Chris has cancer? How could this have happened to him? Why did this happen to such a good boy? Did they get the cancer out of him? Is he going to be okay? When does he get to go home?" They were obviously concerned and scared for me, and worried about my future. I too was apprehensive but sadly, my life was in limbo.

A few days later I was moved out of intensive care. This was great news because it meant that I was healing. I felt so much better now that I was mobile and could see and talk again. Things were looking up and I figured I'd be leaving the hospital soon. I was wrong.

I was transferred out of pediatric intensive care and into the main hospital. I no longer had a private room but a roommate (or two). I was frustrated, now into my third week in the hospital and I was getting a bit stir-crazy. I was not only coping with the side effects from surgery but the constant reminders that I was in a hospital.

The smell of disinfectant and antiseptic was overwhelming. Daily announcements echoed over the intercom system like a never-ending soap opera. Rooms were dreary and uninviting, infamous for the adjustable bed covered with white pillows and linen blankets. The tiny ceiling mounted TV was even worse – you had to strain your neck to watch it.

My living quarters were claustrophobic with hardly any privacy. My roommates were very noisy, staying up very late into the evening, watching TV and telling jokes and jumping on their beds. I often struggled to fall asleep and wondered, "Are these kids actually sick because they certainly don't act that way."

I was surprised but pleased when I was informed of my move to the adolescent ward. This section of the hospital was strictly for teenagers. I was relieved since it was much quieter and I could finally get some rest. I was once again alone, and happy I no longer had to be surrounded by all the noise. I would not be alone for long though, and would cross paths with a boy who would become one of my closest and dearest of friends.

I had just returned to my room after a test when I met my new roommate, Dave. He was unlike my past roommates: he didn't talk much and kept to himself. When I walked towards his bed, I realized why. Dave was lying down in bed, flat on his back, staring straight up at the ceiling. He was in some sort of contraption I later learned was called a halo. Steel rods were fused to his neck and skull, stabilizing his head and neck, preventing him from much movement. I asked him why he was in the hospital and he told me he was recovering from spinal surgery.

Our time together was short, as he wasn't in the hospital for very long, but we formed a friendship during the short time we had. It turned out that we had a lot in common. We were exactly the same age and were both going to the same junior high school. We also lived very close to one another, only one town apart. We bonded very quickly and became close friends. Our chance meeting in the hospital would lead to a friendship that would continue on to the present day, as we have been best of friends ever since.

The worst part of the hospital was the unappealing, flavorless hospital food. Boy did I truly miss eating home cooked meals. Thankfully, my parents brought snacks and picked up food from local restaurants when they came to visit me. I give credit to my sister Tara, who bravely tasted food on my tray even though she didn't have to. I would have refused it as well but that was the diet I was given and I needed the nourishment. I figured the longer I followed the doctor's instructions, the quicker I'd get better and the faster I would get out of this place.

Unfortunately that would not be the case, and I remained in the hospital despite my improved condition and overall recovery. I was eating meals, taking my pills, walking for exercise and resting (when possible) and doing everything required to get healthy again yet I was still unable to go home.

I confronted my neurologist and asked him; "Can I please go home tomorrow? I am feeling so much better." He replied, "Yes Chris, you can go home in the morning." I was so excited and anticipated his arrival the following day to discharge me, but when I saw him again he responded, "I am sorry Chris, but you need to stay a little longer."

I was outraged. I didn't understand why I couldn't go home and I hated him for making me stay. I fully understood keeping me in the hospital if I was sick, but I was better and wanted to leave. I would ask him on numerous occasions if I could go home and he always said the same thing. He told me I could leave and then would take it back. I became very angry with him as my frustrations mounted. He prevented me from restoring normalcy in my life and I wanted to go home and be a kid again, yet I felt like I was in prison.

Days lapsed and I endured countless tests and procedures. School would begin in a few days and I was at my breaking point. I asked my mother, "Am I going to miss school? I don't want to fall behind so early in the year." Hesitantly, she said, "I am not sure Chris. The doctor is busy treating your illness and is not going to risk your health."

I was distraught. I lost the last few weeks of summer vacation due to my illness, and now I could possibly miss school as well. "When am I getting out of here?" I wondered. The first day of school would arrive with me still in the hospital. I was disappointed as I expected to attend the start of seventh grade.

All I thought about was how quickly my life had changed. I went from enjoying my childhood and living life to the fullest, to fighting for my life. My world had changed in an instant. I missed out on my summer vacation and hadn't seen my friends in weeks. Now I would miss school and I had no idea when I would return.

I wondered if my friends were thinking about me, or knew what had happened to me. I was scared about what they would think or say when they saw me again, now with a partially shaved head and a huge scar down the back of my head. Would they be afraid of me and not want to be my friend anymore? Would they no longer want to play with me?

My childhood was at a complete standstill and I was frustrated and overwhelmed. When was I getting out of here? I thought. What would my life be like once I left the hospital? I felt and looked different then I had before surgery. I knew nothing and was scared of what was ahead of me in the coming days.

I suddenly came to the realization that life as I knew it had changed. I began to understand that I wasn't going to just simply walk out of the hospital and resume my normal life. I hated the current condition I was in and resented that my life would not be the same.

I finally snapped, becoming extremely rude and vicious with my words. I didn't care who I offended or upset because they weren't in my shoes dealing with all this heartache. My positive, happy-go-lucky persona changed to resentment, hostility and anger. I became difficult and unreasonable, screaming at doctors and nurses who came to disturb me. I was pissed off and nobody would stop me from acting out. I remember screaming at one particular nurse I had difficulty understanding, "I don't know what you are saying. Get the hell out of here and never come back!"

My parents were unhappy with my behavior and tried comforting me. "Chris you need to be patient," my mom would say. "Things will get better. You need to relax and calm down." My parents were only trying to help me, but they too experienced my wrath. I was tired of waiting around and being the polite, patient, obedient child all the time. I began acting out at my parents, stinging them with words I knew would break their hearts. I'd accuse and blame them for my anguish and pain and say, "You guys don't love me anymore! How could you let them do this to me? The old Chris is dead!"

My timing was terrible, because I was finally discharged a few days later. Suspicion caused me to sarcastically ask my neurologist, "Am I really going home this time?" He replied, "Yes Chris, you are. Your levels have stabilized and you can now be discharged." I was shocked the day had actually come and only believed it when the nurse appeared with the wheelchair to escort me out of my room. "Hooray! I am out of here!" I exclaimed." My thirty-two day stay was finally over.

I was excited to leave the hospital and anticipated seeing my friends and neighbors. The ride home was like a field trip, as I saw sights I hadn't seen in over a month. We pulled up to the front of my house to a "Welcome Home" sign and happy faces. Loved ones warmly embraced me, offering support and well wishes for my safety and recovery. It was a joyous return and a relief to be home again. I looked forward to having fun with my family while recuperating and returning to my old life.

My mother prepared a special meal to celebrate my return home. She asked me what I would like to have when I finally left the hospital. I laughed and told her I would like steak with broccoli and Velveeta® shells and cheese. Needless to say my mother granted my request. That first night home I had a home cooked meal of steak with broccoli florets and a big bowl of Velveeta® shells and cheese!

Neighbors visited the house over the next few days delivering get-well cards and gifts, offering prayers, surrounding me with nothing but love. I was happy to be home again, knowing my hospital days were over and I had survived the surgery.

With the school year already in session I asked my mother, "Can I go back to school now that I am home?" I was excited to see my friends again and catch up on all I had missed from the first week. I was basically back to my old self and wanted to return to school and life as it was before I got sick.

Regretfully she responded, "No Chris you can't. You are still recovering from surgery. You are scheduled for radiation and chemotherapy treatments and won't be returning to school anytime soon." This wasn't what I expected to hear as I figured I could go back to school as soon as I was out of the hospital.

"What?" I painfully replied. "This is not fair!" I was heartbroken. Returning to school seemed impossible. Not only would I miss out on learning but I wouldn't see any of my friends.

I began to think about them, as well as the new friends I had made during the last year and all the opportunities I would miss out on. I couldn't help but wonder, "Will my friends forget about me?" I wasn't sure how long it would be before I could return to school. Then an even scarier thought crossed my mind: "Will I be able to make up the time I missed, or could I end up repeating the seventh grade?"

Mom then dropped another bomb in my lap saying, "Chris, you might have to be home tutored while going through treatments." I raised my arms in the air in defeat and surrendered. "Seriously?" I replied, completely dejected. The news was disheartening as I looked forward to seeing my classmates again. Cancer changed my personal life and now was taking away my social life, interfering in my childhood in the worst way possible.

I had no choice but to remove school from my thoughts for a while. It was more important that I had survived the surgery and that the cancer was gone. I left school behind to focus on what was to come.

A pirate's life for me!

Keep your head up. God gives his hardest battles to his strongest soldiers.

Anonymous

7

Now that I was no longer in the hospital, I began enjoying the comforts of home. I was back in *my* room, sleeping in *my* bed, watching *my* TV. I could go wherever I wanted, no longer confined to a hospital bed. I could eat whatever I preferred, no longer subjected to the hospital diet. I was no longer interrupted by doctors and nurses and focused on resting, recuperation and recovery. Life was moving in the right direction, or so I thought.

Surgery had successfully removed the tumor that grew in my head. Tests proved no more cancer in my body, however radiation and chemotherapy treatments would ensure no rogue cells would spread to my brain or spinal column which could result in future relapse.

I didn't understand why I needed to have more procedures as I was feeling healthier by the day. The headaches had disappeared and the only pain I experienced came from the stitched surgical incision on the back of my head.

I feared the thought of more pain and expressed my discontent to my mother. "Mom, I feel fine and want to go back to school. I don't understand why I need more treatment!" She replied, "The neurologist said there was still a

43

chance of swelling within your brain and the area surrounding your tumor. Any cancer cells remaining have to be eliminated so there will be no future growth or recurrence."

I was too busy venting and complaining to hear my mother's explanation and I honestly didn't care. I wanted to see my friends and play outside and be a kid again. My cancer diagnosis was becoming such an ordeal. "I don't understand. The tumor was removed! Why put me through more precautionary measures?" I was baffled and annoyed.

Doctors were going to do whatever was necessary to prevent my cancer from coming back. Unfortunately, I had no choice but to accept the next stage of my journey and possibly be subjected to more pain and discomfort. I would have to endure additional treatment to rid my body of any possible cancer. Radiation and chemotherapy treatments were immediately scheduled and I would return to the hospital less than a week after my recent discharge. So much for rest and recuperation!

I received chemotherapy in the pediatric clinic once a week for the next eight weeks. I sat for hours in an exam room with an I.V. draining deadly toxins into my arm. I began receiving the drug Vincristine as the first of three drugs over the next fourteen months.

Treatment immediately affected my joints and nerves, causing frequent jaw pain and cramping. I experienced muscle weakness in all of my extremities, and as the weeks progressed I became unable to stand on my own for long periods of time. I took frequent breaks from standing and walking to rest my weary legs.

Radiation treatment began a week later in the radiology ward of the hospital. Mom prepared a series of questions for our first visit to see the radiologist. She asked, "How much radiation will Chris receive? How often will he need it? Are there any side effects to the radiation? What are they? What is going to happen to Chris during the process? Will he get sick?"

The radiologist responded, "Your son will require treatment every day for the next six weeks, each session lasting about five minutes. The side effects may include nausea and vomiting, hair loss, and difficulty swallowing. The treatment could impact your son's growth."

"Did he just say I could possibly lose my hair?" I questioned. "What did he mean it could impact my growth? I could also throw up from this?" I couldn't believe what I had just heard and immediately grabbed my mother by the hand. She pulled me close and held me in her arms.

We were shocked by hearing the side effects and panic and fear pierced my heart once again. I thought, "How was I supposed to get through this? Surgery had only lasted a few hours but now I would need to go for radiation every day for more than a month!

"How will my body respond to the treatment?" I feared. "Will I really lose my hair? Will I stop growing?" I was less than five feet tall when I got cancer, and had not hit my adolescent peak yet. Surely, I had another few inches of growth in my future. The doctor was now telling me radiation could affect my size forever? "Wonderful!" I thought to myself. It felt like just more added stress and anxiety, as if surviving brain surgery hadn't been enough.

My cancer battle had only just begun and treatment vital to my survival was already slowly breaking me down. Chemotherapy began weakening me from the inside, and now radiation threatened my health even further. Reality settled in quickly that I was in for an even bumpier ride, one with much more uncertainty. I wasn't sure what would happen to me now as I prepared for my next battle.

*We cannot change the cards we are dealt, just how we play
the hand.*

Randy Pausch

8

I couldn't begin radiation treatment without some
mandatory preparations. The first was the creation of a special
mold of my upper torso for placement under the radiation
machine. This mold was intended to serve as my positional
cocoon for treatment in the weeks ahead. Its purpose was to
protect other areas of my body from radiation exposure,
focusing solely on my head and spine.

The mold was placed on the exam table beneath the
radiation machine. I would prop my body into the structure,
lying flat on my stomach with my head facing the floor. My
arms stretched outwards over the sides of the table to prevent
exposure. I remained perfectly still while the radiation was
administered to my head and spine. "Sure. No problem." I
laughed. "Let's see how long we can keep the twelve-year-old
still!"

Next, tiny blue dots would be tattooed around the
circumference of my head to assist therapists with aligning the
radiation machine. The treatment plan was to concentrate on
specific locations where the cancer could spread, thus
avoiding any damage to other healthy tissue and body organs.
The toxic rays would destroy anything in the blast radius,
killing both good and bad cells in my head and spine.

I wasn't happy about the idea of permanent tattoos on my head. In fact, I was livid! I voiced my concerns to my mother. "I don't want tattoos! I already have a huge scar down the back of my head! How many permanent marks do I need?" My mother replied, "Unfortunately Chris, the tattoos are necessary for your treatment. You will have weeks of radiation that will need to be administered accurately. I am sure people will not notice."

Mom would be right. The tattoos were so tiny they could only be seen staring directly at my head from a close distance. I felt better the marks were not as visible as I thought they would be. Now that radiation treatment could begin I prayed I wouldn't experience the side effects noted by the radiologist. Unfortunately for me I would.

I walked into the radiation room my first official day of treatment and perused my surroundings. A large machine hovered above an exam table positioned in the center of the room while an oversized garbage pail sat in the corner. I thought, "Well that seems rather odd. Why would they put a garbage can that size in here?" I would quickly find out after my first treatment.

The mold was quite uncomfortable, especially since I had to keep still for so long. I remained immobile with my head pointed towards the floor for close to an hour, but spent only minutes receiving radiation. The skin on my head and back reddened and became irritated as treatments continued. My mother had to apply special ointment with a cotton ball to the area for dryness.

Although exposure to radiation did not hurt, it wreaked havoc on my internal organs. The waves of radiation targeted areas of my brain and spine responsible for balance and coordination and many motor functions controlled by the central nervous system. After a few weeks I began to stumble and bump into things, as my walking became severely unstable.

My stomach grew very sensitive as the radiation made me incredibly nauseous, resulting in frequent vomiting. I quickly learned what the oversized garbage can in the corner was there for. After each session I immediately ran to it to throw up. We became real close, but not in a good way.

As treatment continued, I became incredibly tired and squeamish. I struggled with my walking to the point I could barely stand on my own. I vomited so much it burned my throat, severely diminishing my appetite. Just the thought of food sent me straight to the bathroom.

I remember the day I began losing my hair. I was watching baseball one evening in my parents' bedroom when a commercial came on. I decided to lie back on the bed and relax until the game came on, resting my head in the palms of my hands. I sat up on the bed when the game resumed and stared at my palms. Clumps of hair had fallen off my head! I turned around to look at the bed and saw hair all over the comforter. I yelled to my mother to show her what had happened. She held me while I cried.

I lost a lot of weight as I had no appetite and could not keep down food. To add further insult to injury, I experienced extreme stomach discomfort and bowel trouble. I was extremely malnourished and severely dehydrated from losing so much fluid from intense diarrhea. My insides were literally pouring out of me.

Radiation took ten weeks to complete, instead of six like the radiologist explained. The combination of chemotherapy and radiation decimated my body. I suffered so badly from the effects of radiation that my white blood cell counts dropped. I was admitted to the hospital after my first week of treatment. I stayed in the oncology unit for seven days resting and receiving medicine to raise my blood levels. I even had to continue sessions while in the hospital. I was admitted again two months later.

Weeks of toxic radiation and deadly chemotherapy put me in utter agony as my condition continued to deteriorate. I seemed to be going in reverse. My health wasn't improving but declining! I once again complained to my mother. "Mom, how exactly is this treatment helping me, when it only causes more pain? I thought I was supposed to get better, not worse." Sadly, she would say, "Honey, I wish I could take away all of your pain, but this will help you even though it doesn't seem that way."

I honestly thought I had been through the worst of my cancer but chemotherapy and radiation would prove me wrong. Surgery was nothing in comparison to the beating I took from chemo and radiation. I thought I had surpassed the worst of this disease when it had only just begun. Treatment got the best of me, destroying me from the inside out.

Chemotherapy and radiation wore me down slowly but surely over the next several months. I became a very frail twelve-year-old boy, so weak I could no longer walk the distance from the hospital parking lot to the radiology ward. As my condition worsened, my mother could no longer leave my side and arranged for family and friends to take us back and forth to treatment so she could take care of me.

We were fortunate to have great friends and family supporting us from the very beginning. Mom called upon her best friends for help and they came right to our aid. She coordinated schedules in order to ensure we'd have drivers secured for each week. Even my sixty-five-year-old grandfather drove us to treatment! Neighbors and friends pitched in as well. They took turns watching my sister or filled in last minute to help.

Mom played a crucial role throughout my recovery. Fortunately, she was a stay-at-home mom and was available during the day, unlike my dad who had to go to work. Mom was the one who came with me to all of my doctor visits and procedures, and advocated on my behalf.

I went through three full months of fear, pain, discomfort and extreme exhaustion. When I arrived home after sessions I spent the remainder of the day watching television on the living room couch or sick in the bathroom. I had no energy to move or do much of anything but lie down, watch TV and nap. My nearest and dearest friends were the remote control, an emesis bowl and a box of tissues propped on a plastic tray against the sofa. Talk about exciting times for a young kid!

My first round of Vincristine was finished the first week of November 1988, while radiation continued for another month. Treatment completely transformed my appearance, as I was physically drained and unable to walk or eat. I was extremely uncomfortable and my insides felt like they were going to explode.

I dwindled away to skin and bones as my health continued on a downward spiral. My face began to look worn and withered and I struggled to stay awake. I was so exhausted from treatment I could barely keep my eyes open as I valiantly fought to stay alive.

At the end of my final radiation treatment in December, I weighed in at a measly sixty-three pounds. I had lost thirty pounds since mid-September! It was clear I would not last much longer without proper nourishment and hydration. A second round of chemotherapy would begin shortly and I needed to be healthy enough to handle it. Unfortunately, that was not exactly how I was feeling.

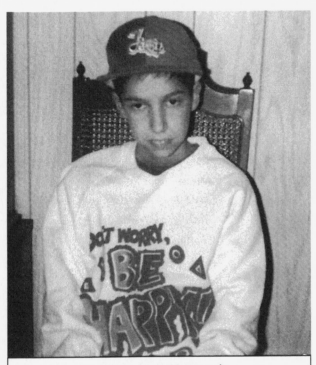

Weighing in at 63 pounds...

Friends don't let friends fight cancer alone.

Anonymous

9

I couldn't stop thinking about school. I felt very depressed and extremely frustrated as I fought this battle alone, while life went on without me. I was troubled I wasn't with my friends and missed out on all the things I loved – my education, participating in school sports, attending dances and seeing fellow classmates. Chances of leading a normal life grew slimmer and slimmer as radiation and chemotherapy broke me down.

Treatment destroyed my body, limiting me physically, mentally and emotionally. The aftermath from treatment left me shattered and completely drained of strength. I was so distressed and looked to my mother for comfort. Tears poured from my eyes as I expressed my sadness.

"Mom, I feel horrible. Look at how much weight I lost! I don't even look like me anymore. How can I possibly go anywhere in this condition when I am a complete mess?" Mom responded, "Chris, you are going through a lot right now. You will get better once treatment is over. We love you so much and are here to help."

It was clear to me now why I couldn't return to school. I had only received a fraction of my treatment and was already struggling and debilitated. I was kidding myself in thinking a return to school was even a possibility. There was no way in my condition I could walk the halls or climb stairs with hundreds of other kids. I couldn't possibly stay in school for an entire day carrying books and a full course schedule when I was so tired all the time. It was inevitable I would need home schooling in order to keep up with my classmates.

My mother contacted the school district and arranged for in-home tutoring for me. This would prevent me from falling behind or getting left back from school. I was happy to hear I could get home schooled. It would be a nice change of pace to be able to do school work and read, not merely watch TV and sleep all the time. Plus, I would see other people and converse with other individuals for a change, not just my mom, dad and sister.

I was excited to start home schooling and anxiously asked my mom, "When are my teachers coming? I can't wait to catch up!" My mother had to reel me in from my sudden excitement. "Chris, they will only be here a few hours a week after school. It will not be the same as normal class."

It didn't matter to me how brief or infrequent they would come tutor me. I was just glad I wouldn't fall behind, and could sustain some kind of normalcy while undergoing treatment.

Four teachers from the Mineola Middle School began tutoring me after school hours. They taught me all the major subjects; math, science, social studies, and English. I had homework to do and tests to take, and learned as much as I could when I was feeling well enough to do school-related tasks.

My teachers were exceptional, dedicating their valuable time to help me finish school. They spent countless hours teaching me coursework and keeping me informed of school events. They delivered messages from friends and get-well cards signed by students and faculty. They were very patient and understanding, repeating subject matter I didn't understand, and allowed me frequent breaks when I got tired or had to use the bathroom when I got sick. Quite often sessions were cancelled early because I just wasn't feeling well.

Overall, radiation and chemotherapy would prevent me from attending school for two whole years due to my frail state and weakened condition! Those were two very rough years for me. I was alone all the time away from my school friends. Friends would try to stop over after school, but that was when I would have tutoring. I turned away late evening visitors because I always felt crummy and exhausted and was not up for company.

A disconnection suddenly began to form in my relationships with friends. On those rare opportunities we hung out I was unable to physically play because I was so weak. I also wasn't in school, so I couldn't identify with anything pertaining to school-related activities or events. I always felt sick, so I never felt up to doing anything or going anywhere. Basically there wasn't much for us to do or talk about, so visits turned out to be very awkward and very brief.

I had become dreary and unexciting —and frankly rather boring —and didn't feel comfortable with my physical self anymore. I certainly didn't want to waste their time, so I would say, "Thank you for coming to see me but you don't have to stay." I lost all of my self-confidence and could no longer interact with my peers anymore. This would dramatically change my rapport with many friends, which became very upsetting.

I was very fond of this one girl in middle school. We became friends in sixth grade and liked each other. She was my first real crush. She was always very kind and friendly, going out of her way to stay in touch with me during treatment. She called me on the phone to talk and invited me to gatherings with friends to hang out. She even visited me at home to say hello.

Regretfully, I let my condition get the best of me. I was so sick all the time and so conflicted about my illness that I no longer wanted to be around anybody. Conversations during those visits only lasted a few minutes before I would say, "I appreciate your thinking of me, but I am not up to hanging out. I am sorry." I would watch her leave and then go to my bedroom and cry, slamming my arms on the bed in defeat, repeating to myself over and over, "She's your friend and you shouldn't have sent her away."

I really liked her, which made it even more painful. I didn't really want her to leave. This caring, sweet young girl still accepted me when I was sick and I pushed her away. It broke my heart because I knew I hurt her feelings.

I struggled to accept my appearance and condition, fearing I'd only bring others down. As much as I wanted to spend time with other kids and have fun, I felt ashamed and embarrassed of how I looked. As much as I desired social interactions with my peers, I instead closed myself off to everyone I cared about. I let personal struggles get the best of me, pinning myself into a corner, something I never intended to do.

This only added to my mental anguish and turmoil, as I worried so much about holding others back that I never considered how it was impacting me. I barred myself from any fun or enjoyment in my life, and ostracized myself from all of my friends. I wound up immersing myself in isolation, into my own solitary confinement. I hated myself so much and resented the person I had become.

Attempts to attend school never seemed to work out. I tried going to English classes at the middle school so I could see my friends and be part of the surroundings. At least for a little while I could put my illness behind me and feel normal and whole, like I belonged there. Mom would wait in the nurse's office for the period to end and if I felt sick, which I normally did, a classmate would get her to take me out of class.

I would cry in the car on the ride home, discouraged and mad. I hated feeling so different and deserted because of my cancer. "This is not fair! Why can't I be normal like all the other kids?" I would scream. I was missing out on a pivotal moment of my teenage life, watching my adolescence slowly slip away. It was hard to accept.

Fortunately, isolation wouldn't discourage me from my studies. I concentrated on school work to keep pace with my peers, and took all my finals at home and passed all of my courses. I attended graduation with my fellow classmates, despite feeling like a complete outsider.

As if I couldn't draw any more attention to myself already, I would be the one to cause a scene during the graduation ceremony. To add to the self-loathing, socially non-existent, personal misfortunes I was already dealing with, I accidently tripped and knocked my graduation cap off my head while receiving my diploma.

The auditorium was packed with proud parents and graduating students. I was one of the final few to receive my diploma based on last name in the alphabet. Mom had attempted to secure my cap before the ceremony by bobby pinning the few remaining strands of hair on my head to my cap.

I was nervous walking across the stage, struggling with my balance and walking, trying to keep my head straight so as not to lose my cap. I shook hands and accepted my diploma from the assistant vice principal and headed off stage down the stairs to return to my seat. I stumbled (of course) on my way down and momentum caused me to jerk forward, pulling the cap away from my head. I grabbed the cap to hold it in place but only pulled it farther away from my head. Both pins came loose from my hair, causing the cap to fall off.

I caught it in my free hand placing it back on my head as fast as I could, but not before exposing my thinning, partially bald head to the audience. I walked back to my chair in tears, completely humiliated and embarrassed of my appearance. I wanted to hide under a rock, never to be seen again.

Nevertheless, I made it through the remainder of the ceremony unscathed. In hindsight, it was a small price to pay as I graduated middle school with my fellow classmates. What a triumphant accomplishment despite the hellish nightmare I was enduring.

Middle school graduation picture.

What lies behind us and what lies before us are tiny matters compared to what lies within us.

Ralph Waldo Emerson

10

I had a few weeks to rest and put on a few pounds since I needed to be healthy and strong enough to complete the second round of chemotherapy. I had lost a significant amount of weight and could not afford to lose anymore or be admitted to the hospital for dehydration. The neurologist recommended surgically inserting a device into my chest to help with my medical and nutritional needs. At first I thought he was kidding, but he was quite serious. Learning I had to go under the knife a second time further irritated me.

"Another surgery!" I shouted at my parents. "When will this be over? I can't take much more of this!" My parents understood my anger and tried to calm me down. My dad responded, "Hang in there son. You have been very strong so far. Don't give up now." Mom added, "This will be a good thing Chris. You won't have needles pierce your skin anymore and you will be fed fluids to keep you hydrated. This will help you."

Despite my displeasure, I realized how beneficial this would be for the remainder of my treatment. I thought, "At least I won't be stabbed with needles anymore and I can stop worrying about keeping food down." As reluctant and unhappy I was to undergo another surgery, I knew this was going to help me. Besides, the doctor said it was a standard procedure, nothing major. I figured, "What can possibly go wrong?"

I entered the hospital a few days before Christmas to have a central line inserted into my chest known as a Broviak catheter. Two thin tubes would protrude from my chest allowing for the insertion and extraction of fluids from my body, pertinent to my improved nutrition and health. I could be fed intravenously through one line and receive medication and fluids from the other. Blood could be drawn from my port, which meant I wouldn't be subjected to countless needles and jabbed like a human pin cushion.

I awoke from surgery tired and sore, my parents and sister close to my bedside. I turned to my parents and asked, "How did the...ouch... surgery go?" I figured the pain was from my recent procedure and just shrugged it off. I continued, "When can I...ouch...go home?" There it was again, but the pain wasn't coming from my chest, but from my side near my ribcage. I was confused. "Why was I hurting in two different places?" I thought.

I then noticed how painful it was to breathe and inquired, "Did something happen during the surgery? Why is it my side...ouch...that hurts when I talk?" I tried sitting up in bed but felt even greater pain along the side of my ribs. Something prevented me from moving around. I glanced over and saw a long tube emerging from the right side of my body to a machine next to my bed. "What is this?" I asked. Mom answered, "Your lung collapsed after they inserted the central line, which required a tube to re-inflate it."

"What the hell happened?" I yelled. "I thought this was a simple surgery, nothing major?" It turned out the "minor" catheter surgery caused my right lung to collapse. I would need to wait for my lung to heal which meant I had to stay in the hospital for a while, forcing me to stay there over the Christmas holiday.

I was furious over the sudden change of events. "What happened this time?" I shouted. "Someone screwed up and I have to pay the price?" My anger suddenly turned to sadness as I realized I would spend Christmas in the hospital! I cried uncontrollably to my family. "I am so sorry. I didn't mean to ruin the holidays for everyone. Why do all these bad things keep happening to me?"

Mom quickly turned the conversation around. "You did nothing wrong, Chris, and this wasn't your fault. It was an accident that came at the wrong time. You have nothing to be upset about." I was going from bad to worse, stuck in the hospital once again unable to move, just like my first surgery. Now I had multiple tubes coming out of my body!

The lung procedure left me exhausted and uncomfortable. It hurt when I spoke, breathed or moved. I couldn't go anywhere or do much of anything but wait for my lung to heal. I would spend the next fifteen days in the hospital and return home after the New Year. What a great way to spend the holidays.

I had looked forward to the holidays for many reasons this year. The past few months had been hell for my family, and the holidays would be the first time we could all relax and enjoy time away from cancer treatments. I was excited about the holiday season; the Christmas decorations, colorful light displays and all the festivities that came this time of year. I anticipated waking up early Christmas morning with Tara to open presents and enjoy time with my family. I truly loved the holidays and was grateful at this point in treatment to be alive to see it.

Now Christmas was taken from me too, and I was disgusted. I figured my family was just as disappointed, as my cancer disrupted many of our plans the last few months. I wondered how my sister felt, as she also loved the holidays and looked forward to them. I hoped she wasn't mad at me for ruining Christmas and her winter vacation from school.

Tara was not upset, much to my surprise. "We can celebrate when you feel better, Chris." she said. "You are more important." I broke into tears, relieved she wasn't mad, but still felt incredibly guilty I ruined the holidays for everyone. My life rapidly spun out of control, destroying and interfering in everything I cared about. Overcome and overwhelmed, I couldn't help but wonder, "What's next?"

We celebrated Christmas in the hospital that year. My sister, parents, grandparents, uncles and aunts visited and spent time with me in the hospital. They decorated my room with streamers and balloons, and we opened presents and enjoyed time together.

I was thrilled to see everyone and wished I could have fully enjoyed the day, but wasn't feeling well and was not up for celebrating. At least we spent the day together as a family and decided to have an official Christmas when I was healthy and home again. We celebrated our family Christmas after the New Year.

I left the hospital in early January of 1989 with a stitched-up chest and re-inflated lung. Now that I had my Broviak catheter, I could receive fluids and nutrition my body desperately needed and not worry about keeping food down due to nausea and a sour stomach.

I began receiving Total Parenteral Nutrition (TPN) for the next six months to put on weight, preventing further trips to the hospital for dehydration. Nurses came to my house and instructed my parents how to prepare the weekly TPN bags. This included injecting additional vitamins and nutrients that supplied even more nutrition to my body.

My father loved me and wanted to help, but just wasn't comfortable with the procedure. Mom was taught how to treat my catheter, sterilize my lines, and administer the nutrition bags. She learned to swab the catheter ports with alcohol to avoid contamination, and flushed my lines with saline solution before inserting any nutritional fluids into my catheter. Fluids traveled from the TPN bag through a long hose. My mother would insert the needle on the other end into my catheter to complete the connection. The bag was then hung on an I.V. pole while fluid dripped into my port.

TPN was administered over a ten to twelve hour period overnight. This meant I was hooked up to an I.V. pole all evening while I slept. It also meant the pole followed me wherever I went. This proved difficult for two reasons. I could only sleep in one position, and required assistance getting in and out of bed. I was so exhausted from recent surgery that I needed someone to walk with me and follow me around. This became tricky when I had to go to the bathroom.

My chest and side were very sore after my second surgery, making it difficult to shout for assistance in the middle of the night to my parents. I could only whisper, "Mom...Dad, I need help," hoping they would hear me. My sister often helped because she was a light sleeper and woke them up for me. Who knows how many accidents were averted thanks to Tara. She was always there to help me in my time of need.

Although TPN was beneficial for my health and improved nutrition, it limited my ability to get around without assistance. Dependency on family for extra help only added to my frustrations. I felt like an invalid, unable to do anything on my own or take care of myself. I couldn't stand, I couldn't walk, I couldn't eat and now I couldn't even go to the bathroom to pee without help! I simply had to accept some loss of independence for now, as TPN prepared me for the second round of chemotherapy.

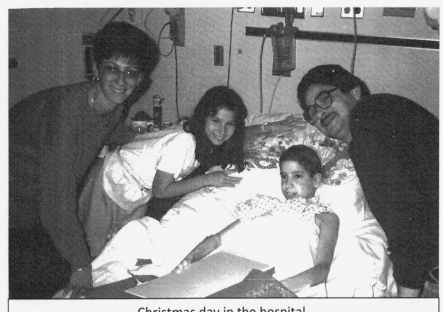

Christmas day in the hospital.

Once you choose hope, anything is possible.

Christopher Reeve

11

Six weeks had passed since I completed radiation treatment, and I felt stronger and healthier as TPN provided the nutrition I desperately required. I now returned to the hospital for more chemotherapy. The nightmare continued.

I was scared to resume chemotherapy treatment, now that I had experienced its fury. Thoughts of more pain and further decline were too much for me to bear. As bravely as I tried to move forward, treatment only pulled me back in the opposite direction. Now I would have to endure cancer's wrath once again: time for phase two.

I approached my mother, troubled and uncertain, terrified of the torture awaiting me once more. I asked, "Mom, how much longer will I need to have chemo? When will my treatment be over?" Mom responded, "Chris, I don't know how long this round of chemo will be, but you have only just begun treatment. In addition to Vincristine, you will receive additional drugs, some much worse than your past chemotherapy and radiation. You are going to have to hang on for a little while longer."

I desperately feared the worst approaching, and wondered how much more my tiny body could handle. TPN helped me put on pounds, but I was still very thin and frail. I was frightened what could happen to my body this time, and

71

still had no clue when treatment would be over. My patience was wearing thin, as well as my desire to continue fighting.

I was so tired and worn-out all the time. I wished this would just end already. I felt like garbage twenty-four-seven and was completely overwhelmed. Falling to my knees I turned to my mother and yelled, "Mom! I can't do this anymore and I want this to stop!"

Vincristine began in the clinic once again, doubling from eight to sixteen weeks of treatment, once again pummeling my tiny body and weakening all my muscles, joints and nerves. I was admitted into the hospital after a few weeks of treatment with a fever. My temperature had spiked so high I spent a week recovering in the hospital before continuing chemotherapy.

My muscles became so weak from Vincristine; severely affecting my ability to walk, that it caused foot drop in both my legs. Foot drop is a condition where the foot falls due to an inability to raise the toes or foot from the ankle. I could no longer lift my feet when walking, consequently tripping and falling forwards. I would visit a prosthetic specialist to have orthotics molded for both my legs so I could walk without falling.

The final two drugs added to my chemotherapy cocktail were Cisplatinum and Lomustine, which were scheduled over the next ten months in eight cycles given every six to eight weeks. Lomustine, better known as CCNU, was known to cause bone marrow suppression, muscle control and coordination damage and speech disorders.

I fortunately did not experience these symptoms, but became quite fatigued, spending much time off my feet. In addition, CCNU caused liver dysfunction and neurological reactions such as lethargy and disorientation. The pill made me very nauseous, causing me to vomit often, further adding to my loss of appetite.

Cisplatinum was the most toxic of the three chemo drugs, requiring overnight stays in the intensive care unit to administer. I received an I.V. drip of the medicine over a ten hour period that battered my insides, creating constant waves of nausea forcing me to throw up every hour.

The toxic drug overpowered my already weakened body. Attempts to sleep were useless, as I tossed and turned in bed, shaky and fidgety from the medicine. I was restless and uncomfortable as treatment slowly dripped into my I.V. I just wanted to get through the process so I would close my eyes in efforts to rest. I refused to watch TV, read or even talk to anyone. I focused on relaxing, awaited the inevitable nausea, heaved and vomited, and then went back to bed.

I returned home the following morning and went to my room to sleep, exhausted and tapped out. I only had a few weeks reprieve before repeating the process all over again. In the meantime, I was still undergoing Vincristine treatment, so there was never a break.

I was once again moving in the wrong direction with my health. It was hard to believe that these medications were actually helping me, when I was withering away to nothing. I became very skeptical of surviving treatment with so many months to go and no end in sight. Who would have thought that exposure to such extreme punishment would be the remedy in beating cancer? I, for one, was feeling it every day of treatment and had to question, "Was all this really making me better?"

I had stopped eating and relied solely on TPN to get me through treatment. This became a concern, as the neurologist feared I could end up in the hospital again for dehydration from malnourishment and lack of appetite. Although TPN was keeping my body nourished, it was not meant to be my only method of nutrition. I couldn't just live on TPN alone and needed to eat real food.

I was placed on the steroid Decadron to further assist with my nutritional needs. Reactions were positive, as I quickly experienced food cravings again. In fact, the medication worked so well I woke up all hours of the night to eat. Decadron increased my appetite so I no longer had to rely on just TPN for nutrition. The steroid also reduced the nausea felt from chemotherapy, which allowed me to eat and keep down food, preventing additional weight loss during treatment.

I surprisingly put on weight, which proved beneficial to my health, but experienced some visible side effects. Most noticeable were external changes to my body, as I began to thicken up and expand like a balloon. I grew rounder and larger, developing chubby, puffy cheeks. I resembled a chipmunk storing nuts for the winter.

Chemotherapy was relentless and unforgiving and broke me down. Any strength I acquired before chemo had disappeared, all my reserves depleted by the toxins ravaging my insides. My counts dropped so low I had to go back into the clinic for a blood transfusion because the medicine made me anemic and weak. I withered away, unable to function.

It was hard staying positive when my ass was being kicked on a daily basis. Every time I thought the worst was over something else came along and knocked me down another notch. I began losing hope and felt like giving up. I hated the life I was living, as well as the person I was becoming. I could no longer look at myself in the mirror. I was appalled and miserable as life only got worse. My health continued to decline, my confidence was at an all-time low and my social life was non-existent.

Months rolled by and treatment continued to wear me down. Chemotherapy destroyed me and I could hardly function. I remember a particular time when the school year was coming to a close, and my mother encouraged me to attend a dance at the middle school. She figured it was a good opportunity to see my classmates one more time before summer began.

I honestly didn't want to go to the dance. I always felt crummy and could never stay for very long and I honestly felt I did not belong there. It was nice to get out of the house and have the opportunity to socialize with my peers, but it was hard for me to interact with my classmates in my condition. I felt uncomfortable, looking and feeling so different from everyone else. I don't know what was scarier in comparison, receiving cancer treatment or seeing my friends during cancer treatment. It was just too hard for me to deal with.

Mom wheeled me into the school gymnasium near the wooden bleachers while I scanned the room for people I recognized. I felt uncomfortable and awkward, sticking out like a sore thumb. I wouldn't be hard to spot entering the room, the only kid escorted by his mother in a wheelchair!

Kids who knew me came over to say "hi," happy I was there. Others stopped over briefly to see how I was doing, than headed back onto the dance floor to join their friends. Some kids sat with me to exchange brief conversation, then walked away to mingle with a bunch of other classmates. I couldn't help but feel so disconnected from my peers.

I had no real relationship with them anymore and honestly felt like the elephant in the room. I sat near the bleachers watching events of the dance unfold, unable to participate, feeling like I did not fit in. I felt like an outcast, having nothing in common with my friends. I simply could not relate to anything happening in school or in their lives, and they couldn't understand what was happening to me.

They were growing up doing teenage things; making new friends, dating, sports, participating in school activities, while my life stopped as I fought to stay alive. We were on completely different paths in our adolescent lives, and as much as I truly desired to have those moments they were way beyond my reach. I skipped over my teenage years straight into adulthood, as I battled for my life at such a young age. I had become an outsider amongst my own classmates and left the dance after an hour.

Mom witnessed first-hand the emotional and physical distress I was under from chemotherapy, especially from the Cisplatinum. By the end of my fourth treatment I was so depleted of strength I could no longer get around without a wheelchair. By the seventh treatment I was practically comatose. Observing me at my absolute lowest, she had seen enough and pleaded with the neurologist. "How much more chemotherapy does Chris have to go through?" She asked. "Hasn't he been through enough already? Does he really need the final round of treatment?" I had basically reached rock bottom. The tank was way beyond empty and I had become deathly ill.

The doctor nodded in agreement. "Chris has had enough Cisplatinum and will not require the final cycle. He will only need to complete the last few treatments of Vincristine. The combination of both radiation and chemotherapy is sufficient at this point in his course of treatment that he can skip the final round of Cisplatinum." Mom shared the glorious news from the doctor and I was beyond happy, so relieved I wouldn't require the last round of chemo. I was at the end of my rope and unsure how much more I could take.

I only had five more treatments of Vincristine, which meant treatment would end soon. "Only three more months left." I said to myself. "Hang in there for just three more months." The finish line was in sight and I couldn't wait to cross it.

I completed my last chemotherapy in November of 1989 and was thrilled when it was finally over. I was overjoyed, however, my beaten frame prevented me from expressing much emotion. I looked like the walking dead and I felt like crap.

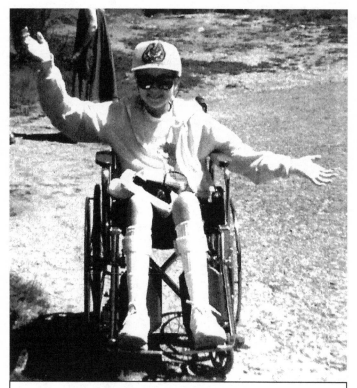

On the road to recovery!

Home school.

I will fight until the end.

Benjamin Franklin

12

I received physical therapy and home care during my last few months of chemotherapy beginning July of 1989, almost one full year from my original diagnosis. I was incredibly weak and tired all the time, unable to walk or get around without assistance. I lost a lot of strength and energy from the toxic chemo entering my body and needed to improve my physical condition from further decline.

I worked with a therapist two to three times a week for the next seven months to improve my overall mobility, concentrating on balance and stretching exercises. It was a long frustrating process as I learned to walk and perform normal everyday functions all over again.

I struggled with therapy for months. Chemotherapy continued weakening my muscles, preventing me from making much progress. I had so much difficulty with balance and coordination that I couldn't perform the simplest of tasks, like walking a straight line or balancing on one foot. I often fell down discouraged and would shout out in frustration. "I can't do this! It's too hard." I screamed at my therapist and parents as I struggled with therapy, as normal functions I once took for granted became complex tasks to perform. The work was demanding and I failed to progress as quickly as I wanted. Chemotherapy was beating me down.

Physical therapy required continuous effort on my part, practicing in-home exercises on my own or with my parents. In jest, my sister took advantage of my lack of equilibrium and purposely bumped into me because she knew I would stagger. We laughed about it because we both knew she was being playful. Tara knew I'd retaliate and push her back - not that she moved much from my push. I knew she missed the brother I once was, and that encouraged me to get stronger.

Tara looked up to me before I got sick. She was my shadow and always wanted to be around me. As siblings we loved each other and played games all the time, put on shows for our parents and goofed around, mostly just having fun. That all stopped the day I was diagnosed.

We were both on separate ends of the family spectrum. I took all the attention from mom and dad while she was transferred from one place to another. I became the primary focus while Tara was brushed aside. Even when we were all together as a family she sacrificed to help me whenever I needed.

Tara and I were always very close. We played together all the time and enjoyed being together. I worried about her and she worried about me. We looked out for each other. She was only nine years old at the time, and I knew she was scared. I didn't see her as often, since she was either in school or staying with friends, while I was going back and forth to treatment. She was having fun playing outside, spending time with friends while I stayed alone by myself in my room and on the living room couch.

Years after treatment Tara and I had a conversation about this difficult time and how it affected her. I wanted to know her thoughts and feelings about the time I got sick. She told me she spoke to my parents about how frightened she was for me, and didn't want me to die because she loved me and didn't want to be all alone without her big brother.

She also said that she was scared that she would get cancer too, and have to go through the same experience that I did. My heart breaks when I think back to that conversation, because she must have been going through so much at such a young age, yet set her personal feelings aside to help me. I love my sister more than words can say.

If I felt sick she was there with an emesis bowl. If I needed help into the bathroom she woke up to tell my parents or gave me her shoulder to lean on. If I ever needed something Tara was always there to assist. She was looking out for me when I should have been watching out for her.

In addition to physical therapy I began receiving home care. Nurses came to my house once a week to check my blood levels and vitals to make sure I was doing ok with chemotherapy, ensuring I wasn't declining or at risk for another admission to the hospital. Thankfully, my counts remained normal as I managed to claw my way through treatment. I continued home care until October of 1989.

Now that treatment was over I could focus on recovery, and began to make steady progress, no longer exposed to harmful chemotherapy drugs. My body happily responded. I felt better and looked forward to the future. With treatment finished, I would return to visit the neurologist for an overall summary of my health.

I had overcome so much since that traumatic day in the neurologist's office back in August 1988. I endured a one-month hospital admission, 32 sessions of radiation to my head and spine, a deflated lung, a chest tube insertion and months of exhausting chemotherapy. In addition, I experienced multiple finger sticks, I.V.s, spinal taps, blood transfusions, bone scans, CAT scans, MRIs, a Myelogram and a bone marrow aspiration.

I was relieved it was finally over and I was free to be a kid. I had basically become a young man, confronting subjects and hardships most children never experience at such a young age. I couldn't wait to resume my life and see what the future had in store for me. I was grateful to have come so far and survived.

Mom made an appointment with the neurologist a few days after all of my treatment had finished. I was excited yet nervous to see him because he would determine my future care. I feared I might need to go through more treatment and just wanted to move on with my life.

We grew really close to the neurologist, as he was instrumental in saving my life. I visited his office dozens of times during my illness and became well known by his staff. We walked into his building, said our hellos and followed the neurologist into his office. We sat down in chairs in front of his desk. He spoke first. "Chris, it is good to see you. How are you feeling?" I replied, "I am doing okay, just very tired. I feel beat up." He responded, "You will feel better over time now that treatment is over."

I got right to the point about my health and asked him, "Am I in remission or could the cancer come back?" He replied, "Chris, do not worry. Your tumor was removed and followed with aggressive radiation and chemotherapy. We have performed many tests and they show no cancer in your body. Your treatment was very successful. Go live your life and be happy." He continued, "The longer you are cancer free the less likely it will ever return."

Mom then asked, "Could Chris experience any future effects from the drugs he was exposed to during treatment?" The doctor acknowledged, "There is a possibility of long-term effects of the drugs but only time will tell. Chris will need to see me for follow-up care on a monthly basis. He will also need to visit the pediatric oncologist as well. We will then spread out his visits to every three months, six months, and eventually once a year, until he will no longer require follow-up appointments. Chris will also need to continue going for MRIs to make sure there is no return of his tumor."

After our discussion I followed him into the exam room. He performed the same examination from our first meeting—walking a straight line, moving towards and away from him, checking my reflexes, strength and breathing. He then pulled out the small flashlight from his pocket and looked in my eyes, ears and mouth. This time there was no cause for alarm, as I was given a clean bill of health.

I returned with him to his office where he announced to my mother that my checkup went well. He said, "I will see you in a month Chris. Be well." My mother walked towards him and gave him a huge hug, thanking him for saving my life. I hugged him as well and cried, grateful for all he had done for me. We said goodbye and walked out the front door.

Chillin' with Tara.

If you change the way you look at things, the things you look at change.

Wayne Dyer

13

I left the neurologist's office thrilled and exhilarated to begin the next phase of my life, but saddened as well. A piece of history remained behind in that office, a chapter forever closed in my life. Aside from occasional MRIs and follow-up visits to the neurologist and the pediatric oncologist, I would hardly see my doctors and nurse friends anymore. I could resume living my everyday life and be a kid again.

I was so relieved, yet frightened at the same time. As excited as I was to go back out into the world and see my friends, I worried how they would react. I worried that they wouldn't like me. I worried my physical appearance would scare them, or they would perhaps tease or laugh at me, or make fun of me since I was different from them. I had been out of school and alone for two years, surrounded primarily by adults and sick children. Now I had to adjust and fit back in with young, healthy kids when I felt so unlike everyone else.

I felt like I had woken up from a long, deep, sleep, unable to identify with myself, nor the world around me. I had taken a time machine into the future, skipping over sixteen months of my life. My cancer experience was so traumatizing and life-changing that the twelve-year-old boy that began this journey had now become a fourteen-year-old man.

I was no longer a child, but at the same time I felt I was...or at least wanted to be. Life had been placed on hold against my wishes while I had to grow-up faster than I wanted. I felt like I had lost a major part of my childhood and jumped right into adulthood before I was ready to mature.

That's when it hit me. I was a frail and withered fourteen-year-old boy robbed of my adolescence, pulled away from my peers and now limited in my physical and social abilities. "What was I supposed to do now?" I thought. I had been under doctors' care for so long I no longer knew of anything else.

I was now forced to pick up the pieces of my so-called-life and move on, no longer the same person I used to be. I simply had no clue what I was supposed to do next and neither did my parents. Cancer didn't come with a "how to" manual, so we had to figure it out on our own. I couldn't help but still feel very afraid.

Support was always provided at the hospital during treatment. We coped and worked through the cancer process from beginning to end with the help of the social worker and psychologist on site. I personally spoke with them quite often during treatment as I had difficulty masking my pain. I couldn't understand why I got sick. Before I was diagnosed, I was attending school, playing sports and loving life, just like any other kid. What had I done to deserve cancer?

I felt like I did something so bad in my life that I was stricken with cancer as some sort of punishment. I felt my childhood had been taken from me and I was robbed of my youth. I was sad, angry, alone and afraid, and desperately needed an outlet to address all the confusion and pain I was feeling. I wanted to share with others all the questions and fears I had. I desperately sought answers so I could move on with my life.

I formed a strong friendship with the social worker and psychologist over the first few months of treatment, and began attending a small support group the psychologist created for young kids fighting cancer. I felt so alone when I first found out I got sick that he thought discussing my concerns and questions with other children could help me.

I met other kids struggling with their illnesses and we voiced our concerns together. Many kids were my age dealing with the same issues. I listened to them as they shared their stories and began to realize how similar we were and that we shared a common bond. We shared laughs and tears together and formed our own support team.

That prompted me to continue seeing someone after treatment ended, so my mother found a social worker who specialized in working with children. My cancer battle had hit me hard during an important phase of my youth and I lost touch with most of my friends. I didn't know how to break through that social wall that separated me from the "normal" kids.

We discussed many emotional and personal struggles I now faced. The question, "Why me?" was a major subject of many sessions. I told the social worker I didn't feel normal and we discussed how I could fit in and get kids to like me again. I wanted peers to spend time with me now that my cancer treatment was over.

Once I returned to school in ninth grade (high school) I found it difficult acclimating to my surroundings and became further withdrawn and depressed. Frustrated, I shouted at my therapist during sessions, "It's so unfair! No one can possibly know how I feel or what I went through!" I think I had every right to feel the way I did.

Another issue consuming me at the time was my own mortality. I felt tremendous guilt and heartache that I was alive, when children I knew from the hospital had died from their cancer.

I had always seen the same kids in the hospital, and we formed friendships. We would visit one another in the clinic and keep each other company while undergoing treatment. My parents formed connections with their parents and supported each other. During these difficult times, we struggled and fought for our lives. It was heartbreaking to hear bad news when a child passed away.

It was very hard to stay positive during treatment when kids I knew were dying from cancer. I couldn't help but wonder how I could possibly ever defeat this disease, and questioned if my battle was hopeless and worth putting in the effort to survive. Was going through all of this treatment pointless, if I was just going to end up dying too? Should I bother to continue fighting any longer since they had lost their battle and I would most likely lose mine as well? Should I just give up and no longer care what happens to me?

Some of my close friends undergoing treatment were not so fortunate. I asked my therapist questions like, "Why were innocent children dying from cancer? What had they done to deserve such punishment? Why was I so lucky to survive?"

The subject was also discussed in conversation with my mother. I figured my mother—the matriarch of the family, the guiding force throughout my cancer journey, the wind beneath my wings, would provide me the explanation I searched for as to why I was still here.

I asked her, "Mom, why did I survive? What did I do that was so special that I lived while others perished? Why am I still here? Mom replied, "I don't know the answer to that Chris. You were very lucky. Be thankful you beat your cancer and are alive. We are all thankful you are still here with us." I responded, "I guess you are right mom. I must be here for a reason, but what? I guess I will have to discover that for myself."

Emotionally, I was at a new low, struggling with the aftermath of cancer. I was re-living the past while struggling with my present physical, mental and emotional state. I was also questioning my future, wondering if I would ever finish high school and someday go to college. Would I ever drive a car? Would I ever meet somebody and fall in love? Would I ever get married, or would I be alone forever?

Despite my triumphant defeat of cancer I was left a tortured child. Everything I knew had changed. I couldn't play the sports I loved so much because I was so small, weak and fragile. I missed two full years of school with my classmates. I lost friends and relationships and became a fraction of the person I used to be. My life was in shambles and complete turmoil.

Nothing good was happening in my life—only pain, sacrifice and constant disappointment. I was alive but nothing seemed to matter anymore and it painfully occurred to me, "What kind of life could I possibly have after cancer?" I felt like my life was in hell and I didn't want to live this way for the rest of my life. Returning to normalcy seemed a lot harder than beating the disease that had brought me to this crossroad.

I wanted to be the twelve-year-old I was before I got sick; running and playing with friends, meeting new kids and having a lot of fun. I simply enjoyed every part of my life. My entire world and everything that meant so much to me was gone and I was crushed. I could not turn back the hands of time.

Now that I was fourteen I questioned what the future had in store for me. Did I have much of a future to begin with? Would I ever get to experience the things I loved and enjoyed so much before I got sick? Could I ever return to the happiest times of my life?

After fighting to live and beat my cancer, I now wished for death. I couldn't handle these new challenges and wanted life to end. I no longer wanted to continue the journey. I had just completed all of my treatment and now succumbed to all the negativity and despair cancer brought front and center.

This is why I am so grateful for the time I spent with the social worker as I was able to find clarity and answers to my questions. I worked with her for over a year and in time began to realize how valuable my life was, and I got my life under control and pointed in the right direction. Therapy provided some well-needed reminders that I was not alone and that my pain and struggles were only temporary at this time in my life. I had just survived cancer, and everything else was minor in comparison. The world was my oyster, and I could pretty much do anything my heart desired!

Music can change the world because it can change people.

Bono

14

Music played a big role in my life before I got sick, and carried me through many hard times during treatment. It was, and still remains an essential part of my life. Music provided diversion from the pain and suffering I experienced during treatment.

I could sing, whistle, or even hum along to music as distraction from my current struggles. I could put on headphones and push play on my Walkman, and focus solely on the beats flowing through my ears, while everything else disappeared.

Music erupted with so much power and expression, exploding with energy and drive. I felt so alive, as music brought out so much emotion I often held from within. I could find a genre of music to accommodate the mood I was currently in, and that always made me feel better.

Mom and I used to listen to cassette tapes on the way to the hospital, and pretended to be DJs, as we swapped out tapes making our own musical arrangements for the trip. Some of my favorites were bands like Skid Row, Bon Jovi, Def Leppard and Motley Crue. I spent hours at home watching MTV and always asked my mom to take me to the music store to buy new music so I could listen to it on the way to the hospital.

I loved listening to popular music of the eighties and slowly gravitated to alternative rock and grunge after treatment ended. I enjoyed bands like Pearl Jam, Stone Temple Pilots and Nirvana. As music evolved, so did my preference as I moved towards the louder, angrier forms of music and eventually began listening to harder rock and heavy metal groups like Megadeth and Metallica.

Personally I found the energy from metal and rock to be exactly what I needed to deal with my struggles, as I was often very angry and the music calmed me down. The thrashing of the guitars and drums piercing through the amplifiers pumped adrenaline into my body and got me swinging my arms and strumming along to melodies. I started playing air guitar and tapping my feet up and down like a drummer banging the drum pedals. I unleashed my frustrations by screaming vocals at the top of my lungs!

Years after treatment and dozens of albums later, I no longer required prosthetics on my legs and walked without any assistance. All that air pedal drumming must have strengthened my feet, curing my foot drop issue damaged by chemotherapy. Music became my new-found friend, as it created entirely new opportunities for me to manage my disease both during and after treatment.

Music followed and helped me through some very rough times and continues to be an escape in times of difficulty. Music provides an outlet unlike any other and still resonates with me to this very day. I always have the radio on or a CD in my car belting out tunes. In later years I have gravitated to progressive metal and classical rock, bands like Rush and Led Zeppelin. All of my friends know I love the band, Dream Theater. Long live rock and roll!

Music fueled the fire inside and therapy eased my pain, and my outlook on life transferred from depression to jubilation. I decided life was worth living and I needed to push forward. I wanted to fight, succeed and live, and did whatever necessary to succeed in my fight. Failure was not an option.

I decided to fight cancer with all that I had. There was no giving up on life for me and I had to beat this. There was really no other choice. I didn't want to succumb to this disease and leave my family. I couldn't leave this world when there were so many things in life I still wanted to experience. I had goals in life to strive for so I decided not to give up. I fought and I fought and I fought. I dealt with all the pain and discomfort and remained positive. I had finally found the silver lining to help me beat my cancer!

So when the time came for any procedures or treatments, I did them willingly. I took my visits and therapies in stride and kept myself going. My cancer battle became a mental test of will and determination and patience truly became my greatest asset!

My battle with cancer transformed me into a soldier of war. I went through hell and back only to come out on top as a hero. My mother later told me I received adult dosages of cancer treatment and that my courage and bravery surprised not just her and my dad, but the doctors and nurses as well.

I had survived it all, and was grateful to be alive. I closed a very important chapter in my life, and was ready to start the next one. It was the beginning of a new me, a Chris 2.0. I enjoyed life again and could finally relax. There was no more pain or discomfort. No more tests or surgeries. No more overnight hospital stays. It was time for me to move on from my past and onto my future.

But first we were going to party! I knew my parents and sister were proud of me and I was glad I was well. I defeated my cancer and it was time to celebrate the victory and all I had accomplished. I asked my parents, "Mom, Dad, could I have a party to celebrate my recovery?" I wanted it not just for me but for my family, who stood by me since day one. I wanted to thank the people that shared my journey; friends, neighbors, doctors, nurses, therapists…everyone. I wanted to show my love and appreciation for all they had done for me. I don't know if I could have survived without their love and support.

My parents felt the same way as I did, sparing no expense for the celebration. I was so excited for my party. We hired a DJ and booked a fancy catering hall in town. Close to two hundred people celebrated with me on my special day. The party took place just before my fourteenth birthday and became my birthday/recovery party. This closed the chapter on my battle with cancer.

My birthday/recovery party. We're ready to dance!

We know that pain can be necessary and heroic. That our difficulties need to be condemned but often seem as a rite of passage that opens doors to greatness.

Brandon Burchard

15

My family experienced a lot over those two years, sharing in this nightmare together. We were looking for an escape from Long Island, somewhere to get away and have some fun. I wanted to hang out with kids again but did not want to feel uncomfortable in the process.

I had endured a lot during treatment and was no longer capable of the physical activities I once excelled in. I still experienced side effects after treatment and was unsteady with my gait. I wanted to spend some quality time with Tara and my parents. They observed me at my worst and now could appreciate me in my better frame of mind.

My mother heard about a camp that catered to the needs of sick children and their families. I figured this would be perfect, since I would not have to feel any different than the other children attending. I wouldn't have to feel embarrassed about the way I looked, nor be alone.

We drove eight hours to Maine and arrived at Camp Sunshine in July of 1989. Camp Sunshine was located on beachfront property near Point Sebago Lake in Maine. Medically trained staff and volunteers lived on site, and a local hospital was nearby in case of emergency. Many volunteers had been campers themselves and faced their own medical adversities. The camp featured many amenities and activities for both children and adults. We were in good hands.

Tara and I spent time with groups of children our own age while my parents engaged in activities with the other adults. I kayaked and played miniature golf and performed skits with my peers at the camp amphitheater. We saw each other for lunch and dinner in the cafeteria, and retired to our own private RV trailer at the end of the day.

We spent evenings on the beach with our counselors sitting by the bonfire hanging out, dancing to music and eating S'mores. It was a wonderful break from the miserable days of treatment and a relaxing getaway for the entire family. It was an amazing week and we met a lot of great people. It was the first of many summer camps in the coming years.

I would attend another camp later that summer, but this time I went alone. Paul Newman's Hole in the Wall Gang Camp was based in Connecticut. My uncle had a house about an hour away from camp, so my family and I slept over the night before.

I had trouble sleeping that night, and was so nervous in the car ride to camp. I had never spent an entire week away from my family before, especially since I had been sick. I knew camp would be fun, but the fact that I would be without them concerned me. Unfortunately, I would let my fears get the best of me.

I never gave camp a chance, as the kids did not look sick to me. I felt completely out of place and very uncomfortable and of course very alone. I was homesick the minute I had arrived and basically shut down and wanted to go home. I had only been at camp a few hours when I told the staff I wanted to leave. They tried convincing me to stay but I would not budge on my decision. My parents were contacted and told to come back and get me. They picked me up the next morning.

We soon discovered another camp that was for cancer survivors and their siblings. Camp Adventure was established by the American Cancer Society in the summer of 1990. Camp DeWolfe of Wading River, Long Island, was renamed Camp Adventure for one week, inviting sick kids and their siblings to enjoy a week of fun near the beach just off the Long Island Sound. Medical personnel and trained staff were present on site and I learned that some of the nurses I knew from the hospital were volunteering. I felt this camp could work out for me.

The American Cancer Society was looking for sick children to attend and I questioned if I should go. "What if this was like the last camp?" I feared. Would I panic and leave again? I didn't want to quit camp for a second time. The idea of spending time away from my parents in my frail condition scared me, but thankfully Tara would be there so I would not be alone. We would bunk in separate cabins but I knew she was close by if I needed her.

I struggled during the first two days of camp. I was still very weak from treatment and found the simplest of activities very challenging. Mentally, I was uncomfortable in my own skin. I was shy and extremely nervous and spent most of my time in the cabin and camp infirmary resting. I felt I could not participate to a satisfactory level so I was uncomfortable and scared to do anything.

Staff volunteers, including my nurse friends, tried to cheer me up. They wanted me to participate with the other kids and get involved in all the fun activities taking place at camp. Unfortunately, those attempts failed. I was so reluctant to interact with anyone or try anything. I figured I would be going home soon enough, but that would change.

Having fun at Camp Sunshine.

Life is tough, but I'm tougher.

Anonymous

16

I was in the camp infirmary when a volunteer came in and noticed me. She said hello and asked my name. She then asked, "Are you feeling ok? Are you sick?"

I responded, "No, I am fine, I just don't feel comfortable being here."

She questioned me, "Are you having fun? Are you enjoying your time at camp?"

I answered, "I think the camp is wonderful, but I just don't think I can do any of the activities. I am always tired and out of breath. I don't want to ruin the other kids' fun."

The volunteer spent the next few minutes speaking with me, encouraging me to come with her outside. "They are playing volleyball on the grass over by the baseball field. Why don't you come with me to watch? You don't have to play."

I replied, "I really just want to stay here. I think it might be best if I went home."

She then pointed outside to a picnic bench about fifty feet from the infirmary. A man was watching the volleyball game. "Would you come outside with me and sit at that table? I want you to meet the man sitting there. He is the camp director, and I think he will convince you to stay."

She was rather persistent so I reluctantly agreed. Together we headed towards the table to meet the camp director. I was glad that I did.

The camp director greeted us with a smile as we approached. We exchanged hellos and sat down while the volunteer introduced me. She then stood up and said. "I have to get back to my post. It was nice meeting you Chris."

I responded in kind, "It was nice meeting you too."

She headed towards the main office atop the hill, while the camp director turned around to speak with me. "I see you met the organizer of the camp. She works for the American Cancer Society."

I was very surprised. "Really! I didn't know that." I responded. "Why is she here?" I asked.

The camp director said, "She works for an organization dedicated to helping people with cancer. She is here because she loves children and wants to help them."

"That is so sweet." I remarked. "She is a very nice lady."

He turned the attention back to me. "Why were you in the infirmary? Are you not having a good time at camp?"

I basically repeated what I had said to the volunteer in the infirmary. We spoke for about twenty minutes, while he listened to me express my fears and concerns and how I felt I didn't belong. He was very caring and I felt very comfortable chatting with him. His jokes made me laugh and I was feeling a lot better in his presence. He wanted me to have fun and enjoy my time at camp.

My attitude began to change the more I listened to him speak. I realized that I did in fact belong. I was just like everybody else attending camp this week and the people here cared about me and wanted me to have a good time. Nobody was going to judge me. They just wanted me to enjoy myself.

He then asked if I would do an activity with him called the pet rock.

"What is that?" I asked.

He replied, "The pet rock is really a simple activity. All you have to do is find a rock that resembles an animal and paint it."

I responded, "Sounds simple enough."

He smiled and said, "That's great. I will go get the paint while you search for a rock."

He headed up the hill towards the main office while I began my search. I explored the camp surroundings for a few minutes and then found a big rock that reminded me of the head of a cobra. The camp director had just returned with various colored paints when I showed him the rock I found. He was pleased and told me to begin painting it. I envisioned the snake in my mind and began to paint.

He sat with me for quite some time, and after an hour I had finished my pet rock—a green snake with purple, yellow eyes and black fangs.

He was impressed with my creation and said, "Chris, it was great talking with you. Thank you for spending time with me. I hope you will stay the remainder of the week with us. I have to leave now and head back to the main office."

Grinning happily I replied, "Thank you for talking with me. I had fun painting my pet rock. I think I will stay a little longer." It was the first time I had smiled all week.

Talking with the camp director made me happy and put me in a good mood. My success with the pet rock got me wondering what I should try to do next. I was ready to do other activities and enjoy camp. I no longer wanted anything holding me back from having fun. Looking back, I can't help but laugh at how something as simple as painting a rock would break me out of my shell.

The pet rock activity provided the distraction I needed to lift me out of my funk. I was no longer worrying whether I could perform tasks or not, I just did them. I wasn't as incapable as I thought, and the activity proved I could still do things. It ultimately became my breaking-out point at camp.

I began playing basketball and board games and interacting with my bunk mates. I enjoyed the activities throughout the week, slowly unraveling layers of self-created fear and uncertainty. I began acting like a kid again.

The conclusion of the week ended with an activity known as Project Adventure. Located in the woods at the back of the camp was an obstacle course built within the trees comprised of ropes, logs, pulleys and ladders. Mind-teasing, group participation activities were assembled to challenge and promote confidence and team building.

As I scanned the course I noticed the quantity and range of obstacles, one more difficult than the next. I looked up and saw that one challenge hovered twenty feet above the ground! I felt sheer terror and my heart started pounding in my chest. I thought to myself, "What were we going to be

110

doing, and how much of this was I expected to try?" Most of the obstacles required physical strength, balance and coordination; abilities I had lost during my cancer treatment. I was also afraid of heights.

"How was I supposed to do any of this?" I thought. This challenge seemed impossible for me to complete and I wanted nothing to do with it. I figured I would be the one to get injured and the staff was crazy to think I could do any of this. Besides, I was scrawny and weak, and there was no way I could balance on ropes or climb trees. This was way too dangerous for me and I would probably break something or really hurt myself.

I quickly voiced my concerns to my cabin leader and the additional volunteers helping on the course. They were very supportive and encouraged me to try my best. Recognizing the positive and motivational value a challenge like this would have on me, they wanted me to attempt it and succeed on the course. I felt safe knowing I would have help along the obstacles and did not want to pass up this opportunity. I figured I had nothing to lose and decided to give it a try.

I remember the words of encouragement from fellow campers and volunteer staff as I approached every challenge. I traversed single logs while holding parallel ropes for stability. I swung from one tree stump to another using ropes attached to tree branches high above the ground. To my surprise I successfully maneuvered many of the obstacles. I was proud for trying and not giving up so quickly.

The final challenge of the day was the monster twenty-footer I noticed upon entering the woods. A tightrope four car-lengths long had been tied between two giant trees, two ropes running parallel alongside. We were strapped into a harness while two volunteers clutched tethered ropes from below.

The challenge was to walk the tightrope from one tree to the other, then back to the center of the rope. We would then let go and descend to the ground guided by staff holding ropes attached to our harnesses. This would require serious physical exertion, especially for someone who could barely walk and wore plastic orthotics on both legs!

Wooden planks were anchored to a tree forming a ladder to the platform above. The climb to the top was difficult, as I could not flex or bend my legs since the orthotics I wore spanned the length of my feet up to my knees. I stiff-legged the entire climb and had to ascend the ladder with my toes pointed out, gripping each plank using the balls of my feet. I was exhausted when I finally reached the top, and had to stop and take a few breaths while standing on the platform. That was tough for me and drained much of my energy but I continued. I still had to walk across the tightrope and descend to the ground.

I took my first step out onto the tightrope shaking uncontrollably, trying to focus. Campers below encouraged me forward as I started toward my destination point, not looking down. Sweat began pouring down my shirt and my legs were in excruciating pain and started to cramp.

Step by step I eventually reached the tree and turned around to head back. I never thought I would get to this point but I still had so much further to go. I felt like I had been up there for hours. Finally reaching the other side, I turned around and headed to the center of the rope to the drop point.

My hands were red and raw as I clutched the ropes for dear life. I refused to release my grip as I prayed I wouldn't lose my balance and fall. Meanwhile cheers continued from below. Campers shouted, "Let go, you will not fall. You can do it Chris." My heart beat increased and my hands continued to sweat as nerves got the best of me. I felt like I was going to pass out. There was only one way down from here.

I took a deep breath and released my hands from the ropes. Volunteers controlled my descent to the ground below, leading me towards the earth. For a moment I felt like I was flying.

Applause and roars of celebration awaited me as I touched the ground with my own two feet. Volunteers shouted, "You did it Chris, great job." I grinned from ear to ear, so proud of my accomplishment. It was a moment I will never forget and an important obstacle for me to overcome personally. It was a strong reminder that I could handle anything standing in my way, just like my cancer. I just had to believe in myself and try and I could conquer anything!

The week became a major victory and huge motivational boost for me in years to come, as I felt more like my old self again. My sister Tara had noticed the changes as well. "Chris, I saw you playing baseball yesterday!" she happily acknowledged. "You haven't done that since before you got sick."

My improvement was clearly seen by the staff as well, as I was named camper of the week. I was given a special plaque for my accomplishment and was interviewed by

Channel 12 news during our final night in Wading River. I was so excited to call my parents to tell them I would be on television. I was so happy and proud of myself. A few weeks later I would be interviewed again, this time with the camp director at the Channel 12 news studio. My camp experience had run full circle as I was once again sitting alongside the gentlemen who made it so worthwhile in the first place.

Camp Adventure.

It ain't how hard you hit… it's how hard you can get hit and keep moving forward. It's about how much you can take and keep moving forward.

Rocky Balboa

Rocky

17

Cancer completely transformed my life, disrupting my childhood at an important stage of my adolescence. I was subjected to intense pain, suffering, heartache and severe mental, emotional, and physical trauma. Yet despite all of the misery and despair, it *did not* beat me!

I was fortunate to meet so many wonderful people on my journey. So many individuals gave their time, support and love to help me conquer my cancer. I learned about true friendship and was blessed to be surrounded by so many caring people.

I realized how strong a person I was and that I could conquer anything thrown my way. I learned about determination and drive; to never give up and to always move forward. I learned to be patient and to accept life as it comes. Most importantly I learned that family sticks with family, and to appreciate the time I have with them.

Camp reignited a flame that had burned out two years before. I began to realize how precious a gift life was, and to be thankful for each day I have on this earth. Cancer may have taken two years of my life, but it gave me clarity and understanding for things I had taken for granted.

I would not have met one of my dearest and closest friends if I hadn't gotten sick. I wouldn't have had the opportunity to meet some famous celebrities like Kenny Rogers, Kaity Tong and Kathy Lee Gifford. I would not have seen the New Kids on the Block in concert. I may never have gone to camp or become camper of the week.

As a survivor, I was able to talk to an audience of physicians and health care providers to bring more awareness about childhood cancer. I was fortunate to help fight the war by sharing my experiences with others for the purpose of education and understanding of the disease. I once again have the chance to help inspire others by writing this book.

In 1993, I was honored by the American Cancer Society and received the Courage Award for bravery and perseverance in my cancer battle. I would go to Albany and speak in front of a crowd of cancer supporters. I even met the governor's wife and had lunch with her.

My appetite was still poor at the time and I was turned off by the food offered at the event. The governor's wife noticed I wasn't eating and asked her personal chef to make me pasta. It was so thoughtful and considerate of her because she knew that was something I would eat. It was a wonderful tribute and honor to receive the award.

My favorite moment by far was meeting my favorite horror villain. During treatment I learned of organizations that provided wishes to children suffering life-threatening illnesses. I became very excited and began thinking about my own wish.

"What should I ask for?" I thought. "Should I ask for a new bike or a video arcade game? Maybe I should wish for a vacation to Florida to go to Disney World?" I spent weeks thinking about what I wanted as it was so hard to decide. I knew it had to be something I would never forget.

The wish I decided upon was the first of its kind. I was a big fan of horror movies before I got cancer, and grew fond of a particular evil doer known for his burned skin, red and green sweater, fedora hat, and glove of knives. I wanted to meet the celebrity Robert Englund, who played Freddy Krueger in the *Nightmare on Elm Street* movies.

My wish was granted by the Starlight Children's Foundation and my family and I were flown to Los Angeles, California to meet Robert Englund. The trip became a family vacation as my uncle lived in Los Angeles, so we stayed with him for a portion of our visit.

We got to see how game shows like *Concentration* and *Jeopardy* were shot for syndication, and spent three days in the Disney theme parks, visiting Epcot Center, Hollywood Studios and Disneyland. I have so many great memories of that trip.

I was so nervous to meet my horror idol. I was accompanied by my parents and sister to meet him. I prepared my outfit appropriately, wearing a Freddy Krueger shirt of course. I was given a replica of Freddy's fedora hat and plastic glove by the representative of the Starlight Foundation upon my arrival at the Hard Rock Café, one of the many gifts I received that day.

I was particularly concerned how I'd feel physically, as I still dealt with poor appetite from treatment. I was afraid I would just sit with him, not eating anything when we met.

Robert Englund showed up shortly after our arrival at the Hard Rock Cafe. He was alone, no security or limo or anything. I was thrilled to get to meet and talk with him.

I was very comfortable around him and even ate my lunch. He was very friendly and brought along some cool Freddy photos from *Nightmare on Elm Street* movies that he personally signed for me. He even wrote some clever Freddy sayings on them, like "see you in your dreams" and "take a nap, punk."

He brought along Freddy Krueger portraits he had personally received from fans from around the world and gave them to me! I still have them to this day framed and in a safe place. He took photos with my family and hung out for a few hours before he left. It became a dream come true and a great family vacation. It was a once-in-a-lifetime opportunity and something I will never forget.

In recent years I have attended a long-term care program for cancer survivors run by doctors and nurses who treated me when I was a kid. I was given all of my medical information from my cancer treatment, which came in handy for reference in my adult years with visits to new doctors. Since I was one of their child survivors I had the opportunity to be part of a magazine shoot for an article focusing on aftercare for long-term cancer patients. It was pretty cool and I was honored to be asked to participate.

My first shave! Wish fulfilled!

Enjoying vacation with family in California.

All we have to decide is what to do with the time that is given to us.

Gandalf the Grey

Lord of the Rings- the Fellowship of the Ring

JRR Tolkien

18

The threat to my personal health at such a young age has influenced my life's journey ever since I got cancer. Survivors can't help but think about relapse or recurrence, and cope with long-term side effects from their treatment.

My hair never grew back the same way after treatment was over and thinned as I got older. I did attempt wearing a custom-made wig, but found it uncomfortable and required a lot of up-keep. When I met my future wife Christine, I decided to embrace the real me, so I shaved off all of my hair and grew a moustache and goatee.

I became near sighted in high school and have worn glasses ever since. Damage to my thyroid gland from radiation and chemotherapy requires me to be on maintenance medication for the rest of my life. My high-pitched hearing was affected as well and I now wear hearing aids.

My balance is still unstable, and I have occasionally tripped over my own two feet or bumped into a wall every now and again. I pray I never get pulled over by a cop and asked to walk a straight line!

I went to C.W. Post College and graduated with a Masters degree in Public Administration with a concentration in Healthcare. I have worked in home care for a local hospital and spent years in health insurance.

I have volunteered and participated in the American Cancer Society's Relay for Life events, raising money for a cure for cancer. I contribute donations to fund research in efforts to help stand up to cancer. I have lived strong and celebrated twenty-eight birthdays since my cancer battle ended. I am now forty years old.

In hindsight, I cannot recall a time in my life when cancer has not followed me. It should be no surprise that it does to this very day.

I have spent the past two years studying at the Institute for Integrative Nutrition® and became a Certified Health Coach, focusing on the overall health and well-being of cancer survivors. What a shocker, right? I have created my own website and business dedicated to helping others, and I am excited to see what is to come along this new path.

My logo is a tree symmetrically divided into two halves, black and green. The green half embodies good health and longevity, positivity and good, while the black half represents the opposite; sickness and instability, negativity and despair.

The tree halves are mirror images symbolizing the importance of balance in life. The branches curve inward towards the center of the tree to form the shape of a heart, representing love. I thank my uncle Wayne for creating my vision.

I named my business, We Cancer-vive + Thrive, because cancer does not mean the end. We can fight hard in battle to overcome adversity and come out on top. We can flourish in our lives for years to come, making all of our dreams come true. We can take initiative and motivate ourselves to conquer obstacles standing in our way, making positive strides towards a happier, healthier future.

In my quest to overcome cancer I endured many hardships, trials and tribulations. I could have given up hope. I could have quit but I didn't. I realized how strong I truly was and that life was worth living.

My life was and *is* important, and family, friends and my support team helped me realize there was more to my life than my disease. I was determined to take my life back and fought through the pain knowing there was a light at the end of the tunnel. There would be an end in sight and I needed to stay positive and carry on.

We are all survivors, living each day, struggling to follow the right course and do the right thing. We try to stay on top of our game and get the most out of life but it is not always easy. There will be obstacles to face and hardships to endure. Bumps will emerge in our path and we will face them head on, dusting ourselves off and picking ourselves up.

Cancer is ruthless and the most difficult thing I personally have ever faced. I hope no one ever experiences cancer's wrath but I find comfort that it can be defeated. Decades later, I am still here, still fighting… still surviving… still thriving.

Speaking at the ACS breakfast conference.

Courage Award speech at the Governor's Mansion in Albany.

College graduation day. Long Island University - C.W. Post.

Relay For Life.

Wedding day.

My girls - Fifi and Gretel.

Courage is being scared to death, but saddling up anyway.

John Wayne

About the Author

Christopher Spevack received his MPA in Public Administration with a concentration in Healthcare from Long Island University – C.W. Post Campus in New York. He is a Certified Health Coach through the Institute for Integrative Nutrition® and a member of the American Association of Drugless Practitioners. He is a long-term cancer survivor of a brain tumor for more than 25 years, and strives to inspire and motivate individuals with cancer by sharing his personal story. He currently resides in Holbrook, New York with his wife Christine and two dogs, Fifi and Gretel.

www.wecancerviveandthrive.com